Crossway Bible Guide

Series editors: Ian Coffey (NT), Stephen Gaukroger (OT)
New Testament editor: Stephen Motyer

Also in this series
Exodus: Stephen Dray
Leviticus: Derek Tidball
Joshua: Charles Price
Ezra and Nehemiah: Dave Cave
Psalms 1–72: Alan Palmer
Isaiah: Philip Hacking
Six minor prophets: Michael Wilcock
Haggai, Zechariah and Malachi: John James
Mark: David Hewitt
1 Corinthians: Robin Dowling and Stephen Dray
Ephesians: Stephen Motyer
Philippians: Ian Coffey
Timothy and Titus: Michael Griffiths
1 Peter: Andrew Whitman

Acts: Crossway Bible Guide

Stephen Gaukroger

Crossway Books Leicester

CROSSWAY BOOKS
38 De Montfort Street, Leicester LE1 7GP

© 1993 Stephen Gaukroger

First edition 1993
Second edition 1997

First published 1993

British Library Cataloguing in Publication Data

A catalogue record for this book is available from the British Library.

ISBN 1–85684–163–4

Set in Palatino

Typeset in Great Britain by Parker Typesetting Service, Leicester

Printed in Great Britain

CONTENTS

Welcome!

These days, meeting together to study the Bible appears to be a booming leisure-time activity in many parts of the world. In the United Kingdom alone, it is estimated that over one million people each week meet in home Bible-study groups.

This series has been designed to help such groups and, in particular, those who lead them, but they are also eminently suitable for individual study. We are also aware of the needs of those who preach and teach to larger groups as well as the hard-pressed student, all of whom often look for a commentary that gives a concise summary and lively application of a particular passage.

We have therefore enlisted authors who are in the business of teaching the Bible to others and are doing it well. They have kept in their sights two clear aims:

1. To explain and apply the message of the Bible in non-technical language.
2. To encourage discussion, prayer and action on what the Bible teaches.

All of us engaged in the project believe that the Bible is the Word of God – given to us in order that people might discover him and his purposes for our lives. We believe that the sixty-six books which go to make up the Bible, although written by different people, in different places, at different times, through different circumstances, have a single unifying theme: that theme is

Salvation. This means free forgiveness and the removal of all our guilt, it means the gift of eternal life and it means the wholeness of purpose and joy which God has designed us to experience here and now, all of this being made possible through the Lord Jesus Christ.

How to use this Bible Guide

These guides have been prepared both for personal study and for the leaders and members of small groups. More information about group study follows on the next few pages.

You can use this book very profitably as a personal study guide. The short studies are ideal for daily reading: the first of the following questions is usually aimed to help you with personal reflection (see *How to tackle personal Bible study*). If you prefer to settle down to a longer period of study you can use groups of three to five studies, and thus get a better overview of a longer Bible passage. In either case using the Bible Guide will help you to be disciplined about regular study, a habit that countless Christians have found greatly beneficial. (See also *How to tackle Acts* for methods of selecting studies if you do not intend to use them all.)

Yet a third use for these Bible Guides is as a quarry for ideas for the busy Bible teacher, providing outlines and application for those giving talks or sermons or teaching children. You will need more than this book can offer of course, but the way the Bible text is broken down, comments offered and questions raised may well suggest directions to follow.

How to tackle personal Bible study

We have already suggested that you might use this book as a personal study guide. Now for some more detail.

One of the best methods of Bible study is to read the text through carefully several times, possibly using different versions or translations. Having reflected on the material it is a good discipline to write down your own thoughts before doing anything else. At this stage the introduction of other books can be useful. If you are using this book as your main study resource, then read through the relevant sections carefully, turning up the Bible references that are mentioned. The questions at the end of each chapter are specifically designed to help you to apply the passage to your own situation. You may find it helpful to write your answers to the questions in your notes.

It is a good habit to conclude with prayer, bringing before God the things you have learned.

If this kind of in-depth study is too demanding for you and you have only a short time at your disposal, read the Bible passage, read the comments in the Bible Guide, think round one of the questions and commit what you have learned to God in a brief prayer. This would take about fifteen minutes without rushing it.

How to tackle your group Bible study

1. Getting help

If you are new to leading groups you will obviously want to get all the help you can from ministers and experienced friends. Books are also extremely helpful and we strongly recommend a book prepared by the editors of this series of Bible Guides: *Housegroups: the leaders' survival guide*: edited by Ian Coffey and Stephen Gaukroger (Crossway Books, 1996). This book looks at the whole range of different types of group, asking what is the point of it all, what makes a good leader, how to tackle your meeting, how to help the members, how to study, pray, share, worship and plenty of other pointers, tips and guidelines.

This book is a 'must' for all leaders of small groups. It is written by a team of people widely experienced in this area. It is available at your local Christian bookshop. If you have difficulty in obtaining a copy write to Crossway Books, Norton Street, Nottingham, NG7 3HR, UK.

2. Planning a programme with your Bible Guide

This guide is a commentary on God's word, written to help a group to get the most out of their studies. Although it is never ideal to chop up Scripture into small pieces, which the authors never intended, huge chunks are indigestible and we have tried to provide a diet of bite-sized mouthfuls.

If you want to get an overview of the Bible book in a series of meetings you will need to select appropriate studies for each meeting. Read them yourself first and prepare a short summary of the studies you are tackling for your group. Ideally you could write it on a sheet of A5 paper and hand a copy to each member.

Do not attempt to pack more than one study into one meeting but choose the crucial one, the study which best crystallizes the message. There are examples in *How to tackle Acts* below.

If you do not intend to cover the whole Bible book, choose a series of studies to suit the number of meetings you have available. It is a good idea to use consecutive studies, not to dodge about. You will then build up a detailed picture of one section of Scripture. Alternative examples of programmes of study for this book are given in *How to tackle Acts*.

3. Resources

You will find any or all of these books of great value in providing background to your Bible knowledge. Put some of them on your Christmas list and build up your library.

New Bible Dictionary or *New Concise Bible Dictionary* (IVP)
New Bible Atlas (IVP)
New Bible Commentary (21st Century edition) (IVP)
Everyday Life in Bible Times: John Thompson (IVP)
The Bible User's Manual (IVP)
The Lion Handbook to the Bible (Lion Publishing)

The Message of the Bible (Lion Publishing)
NIV Study Bible (Hodder & Stoughton)
The Bible with pleasure: Stephen Motyer (Crossway Books)

The relevant volume in the IVP Tyndale Commentary series will give you reliable and detailed help with any knotty points you may encounter.

4. Preparing to lead

Reading, discussing with friends, studying, praying, reflecting on life . . . preparation can be endless. But do not be daunted by that. If you wait to become the perfect leader you will never start at all. The really vital elements in preparation are:

▶ prayer (not only in words but an attitude of dependence on God, 'Lord, I can't manage this on my own')

▶ familiarity with the study passage (careful reading of the text, the Bible Guide study and any other resource books that throw light on it) and

▶ a clear idea of where you hope to get in the meeting (notes on your introduction, perhaps, recap what was covered at the last meeting, and what direction you hope the questions will take you in – don't force the group to give your answers).

Here is a short checklist for the busy group leader:

Have I prayed about the meeting?
Have I decided exactly what I want to achieve through the meeting?
Have I prepared the material?
Am I clear about the questions that will encourage positive group discussion?
Am I gently encouraging silent members?
Am I, again gently, quietening the chatterers?
Am I willing to admit ignorance?

Am I willing to listen to what the group says and to value their contributions?

Am I ready not to be dogmatic, not imposing my ideas on the group?

Have I planned how to involve the group in discovering for themselves?

Have I developed several 'prayer points' that will help focus the group?

Are we applying Scripture to our experience of real life or only using it as a peg to hang our opinions on?

Are we finding resources for action and change or just having a nice talk?

Are we all enjoying the experience together?

How to tackle *Acts*

Now let's assume you are planning an eight-week course of studies (you will have to make the adjustments if you have more or fewer meetings). Where do you begin? This is entirely up to you and your group of course but, to get you started, here are a few possible routes you might take.

1. A brief survey of the whole book

There is so much in the book of Acts that no short series of eight studies could properly represent its message. However eight sessions are better than none at all. You may wish to make your own selection (being careful to avoid bias in your choice). Do not select all the readings on the Holy Spirit nor concentrate exclusively on evangelism nor the battle between backward-looking Jews and the new faith, unless, of course one of these is a specific focus for your study. But beware of pretending that any one narrow theme represents the book as a whole.

Here is one possible selection:

2:1–13	The Holy Spirit is released
2:37–47	The growing church

7:51 – 8:8	Stephen martyred
9:1–19	Saul's U-turn
10:23–48	Gentiles are God's people too!
13:13–41	Paul announces good news
24:1–27	Paul on trial
27:27 – 28:10	Shipwreck and Salvation

2. A missionary journey and its consequences

What is often known as the 'first missionary journey' could be covered in the eight studies from Acts 12:19 to 15:34.

3. Focus on Peter

The third possible scheme covers much of Peter's ministry:

2:14–28	4:1–12	10:1–23	11:1–18
3:1–10	8:9–25	10:23–48	12:1–19

4. Focus on Paul

The choice here is much wider but here is a possible selection:

9:1–19	12:19 – 13:3	20:17–28	28:11–22
9:19–43	13:13–41	22:1–21	28:23–31

These outlines are meant to be springboards for your own ideas, so please do not follow them slavishly. Adapt them for your own use, merge them or ignore them. In any case much of Acts will go unread if you concentrate only on these short snippets. You as leader will need to read carefully the whole book so that you can refer your group to sections they have not read. It would be wise to read a whole chapter when studying a part of it – the context often throws light on the verses you are looking at.

What can we expect to learn from *Acts*?

So what can we expect to gain from studying these events which happened long ago? Much has changed in the last twenty centuries but today's churches share some basic similarities with those of the early church. In studying *Acts* we can learn:

▶ That God is alive and still working actively in his churches (including our own!).

▶ That the church has never been perfect.

▶ How to undertake successful missionary work.

▶ How to survive as a church under pressure.

▶ How to use and share gifts and leadership skills.

Finding your way round this book

In our Bible Guides we have developed special symbols to make things easier to follow. Every study therefore has an opening section which is the passage in a nutshell.

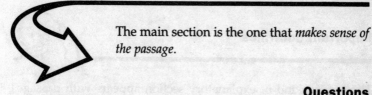

The main section is the one that *makes sense of the passage*.

Questions

Every passage also has special questions for personal and group study after the main section. Some questions are addressed to us as individuals, some speak to us as members of our church or home group, while others concern us as members of God's people worldwide. The questions are deliberately designed:

▶ to get people thinking about the passage

▶ to apply the text to 'real life' situations

▶ to encourage reflection, discussion and action!

As a group leader you may well discover additional questions that will have special relevance to your group, so look out for these and note them in your preparation time.

Digging deeper

Some passages, however, require an extra amount of explanation, and we have put these sections into two categories. The first kind gives additional background material that helps us to understand something factual. For example, if we dig deeper into the gospels, it helps us to know who the Pharisees were, so that we can see more easily why they related to Jesus in the way they did. These background sections are marked with a spade.

Important doctrines

The second kind of explanatory section appears with passages which have important doctrines contained in them and which we need to study in more depth if we are to grow as Christians. Special sections that explain them to us in greater detail are marked with a face as above.

THE WORLD OF THE BOOK OF ACTS

Acts 1:1-5

The story continues

The early Christians had all seen Jesus in the flesh, but they needed his power to do his work. We still need his power 2,000 years later.

Luke wrote his gospel and then turned his attention to writing a sequel – The Acts of the Apostles. Having told Theophilus (meaning 'friend of God') all about the life of Jesus he now wants to update him on all the exciting developments which have taken place since he wrote last. Theophilus was probably not a Christian, but someone Luke knew, who was fascinated by all he had heard about Jesus. He may have been a senior Roman official: Theophilus may even have been a code-name to disguise his true identity. What we do know is that, having whetted his appetite telling Theophilus about Jesus, Luke now goes on to tell him about the impact of Jesus' followers. Acts is their exciting story!

Luke is at pains to point out the link between volume I (Luke) and volume II (Acts). The link is Jesus. He does not just leave his disciples in the lurch, he gives clear instructions about what they are to do when he has gone. Not only that, but for over a month he keeps turning up just to reassure them. The resurrection is no 'flash-in-the-pan' experience, a glimpse of Jesus in an unexpected moment: Jesus is alive! This is no phantom or figment of the imagination:

▶ the disciples see him (verse 3)

▶ he teaches them (verse 2)

▶ he eats with them (verse 4).

This is not 'normal' behaviour for a ghost or hallucination!

On top of all this Jesus makes sure that they are aware of the resources that are available to them. 'Don't go charging off into ministry before you are equipped' he says. He reminds them that John the Baptist knew that his baptism was only half the story (Mark 1:8). He sends them home to receive the best half!

So these anxious followers are meant to be reassured by the *teaching* of Jesus, the *presence* of Jesus and the *power* of Jesus. Christians at the end of the twentieth century have these same three resources available to them. Those first disciples faced losing their leader and friend. When we face 'loss', of whatever kind, we can draw strength from the teaching, presence and power of Jesus. We can receive these blessings through personal prayer, the support of a home group and in the regular services of the church.

Questions

1. 'Many convincing proofs' (verse 3). What evidence is there for the resurrection of Jesus?
2. Do I know the power of the Holy Spirit in my life? How can I experience him?
3. Think of a lonely or sad person in your church. How can you

help them to draw on the resources which this passage describes?

Background to Acts

The book of Acts seems to be the second part of a two-volume work by Dr Luke. The style, grammar and approach of both parts are similar and the 'dedication' is to the same person – Theophilus (Luke 1:3; cf. Acts 1:1).

It was written over a number of months (or years?), becoming available to the church between AD 65 and 70. The story of Acts begins with the ascension, around AD 30, and covers the next 32 years of early church history until AD 62, ending with Paul spending two years under house arrest.

The first half of the book is dominated by Peter, the second half by Paul. With its 28 chapters and 1,007 verses Acts is one of the longest books in the New Testament.

Introducing Luke

Luke appears three times in the New Testament. From these references we learn that he was a medical doctor and a close friend of Paul (Colossians 4:14). Paul obviously saw Luke as an important part of his ministry team, a Christian worker as well as a friend (Philemon 24) and valued as a colleague who remained faithful even when others left (2 Timothy 4:11).

Luke was a Gentile Christian who seems to have been a well educated man with a real heart for mission. Probably first called in when Paul needed medical help, he became much more than a personal physician – perhaps the first missionary doctor. His modesty is such that he avoids mentioning himself in either his gospel or in Acts.

We have very few details about the life of Luke apart from the brief references already mentioned. There is some evidence to suggest that he died, aged 74 years, in the region to the south of the Black Sea. What we do know is that without him we would be almost totally ignorant about the early church and its mission.

Acts 1:6–11
Power to tell others

The disciples needed their focus to be changed and their lives to be renewed. This was a key to mission then – and it still is today.

The disciples were asking the wrong question. Jesus did not have a narrow nationalistic agenda. He was not about to boot out the Romans and establish his followers as the ruling government of the day. Some of his followers were still wanting positions of influence in an earthly kingdom (Mark 10:35–41). Was this when Jesus was planning his coup? Even after all this time with Jesus they are still missing the point. He keeps explaining to them about the kingdom, trying to get it into their heads that his kingdom is bigger than all their political, religious and cultural expectations. Their relatively small concerns would be handled by God the Father, in his own time and way. They were not to worry about the timetable.

Jesus tries to shift their focus back to the business of life in *his* kingdom. When the promised power arrives, they will be able to spread the news of this kingdom all over the world. In his typically direct manner Jesus challenges and envisions in the same sentence. They are to tell their friends and family in the locality, but not be limited to this. They, and their fellow believers, will go all over the planet, telling what they know about Jesus and his kingdom.

Jesus then leaves them. This remarkable scene ensures that these early followers did not think that Jesus just wandered off somewhere and died in obscurity. No, the miracle of the resurrection is followed by the miracle of the ascension. No doubt the disciples were completely mesmerized by this amazing sight and were glad of the angelic words of reassurance. 'Do not stand about staring into space, Jesus is in heaven and will come back to earth some time in the future.' This message from the angels confirms the reality of heaven and the amazing truth that their friend and master is not finished with the earth. Another trip is planned!

This passage promises power for their missionary task. It reminds us – in the very last words of Jesus – what our focus as Christians is meant to be: telling the world about Jesus. Other concerns may be important, this concern is vital. These verses also remind us of where Jesus is now: with his Father in heaven. Heaven is our final destination also and Jesus is one day coming back to take us to heaven with him (John 14:1–4).

Questions

1. Do you get excited about heaven? What are you most looking forward to?
2. In the light of this passage, how would you assess your church's priorities? Where does evangelism come?
3. '. . . ends of the earth' (verse 8). Do you support an overseas missionary? How can you encourage your church to give more money/prayer to foreign mission?

Resurrection

The resurrection of Jesus is a major emphasis in the book of Acts. Acts opens with an appearance of the risen Jesus (1:3–9) and the rest of the book is peppered with references to his resurrection. Peter finds it difficult to preach a sermon without mentioning it (e.g., 2:24; 3:15) and Paul's preaching is similarly influenced by this fact (e.g., 13:30; 17:31; 26:23). For both men, the resurrection demonstrates the reliability of the messenger (Jesus) and the message (the gospel).

Peter and Paul follow this up in their letters, where they see the resurrection of Jesus as central to the Christian faith and its outworking in Christian discipleship (1 Corinthians 15:14; 1 Peter 1:3).

Acts does not present arguments in order to prove the resurrection, it simply accepts it as a fact. For those who had seen, touched and spoken with Jesus, the issue was beyond doubt.

Evangelism

The first Christians saw evangelism as a natural response to their own conversion, based on a command from Jesus (1:8; cf. Matthew 28:18–20). Only Philip is actually described as an evangelist (21:8) and this is to distinguish him from Philip the apostle (1:13) rather than to indicate a formal title.

Sharing the good news was seen as the responsibility and privilege of everyone. Apostles evangelized (Peter and John), prophets evangelized (Barnabas), teachers evangelized (Paul) and even deacons evangelized (Stephen and Philip)! Telling others about Jesus seems to be a very high priority; it is the focus of almost every chapter in Acts.

This is even more remarkable when you consider the pressure they were under to be silent. Faced with this kind of opposition, most of us would be content to let evangelism slip down our list of priorities.

Acts 1:12–26

Waiting for God to act

Obedience to God often involves waiting; and waiting involves prayer.

Down from the mountain-top (verses 12–14)

The disciples took the one-kilometre journey back to base in Jerusalem. It was a relatively short walk, though perhaps over rocky or steep terrain. It was a very long journey emotionally however, back from the mountain-top experience of the ascension into the valley of city life. They congregated in an upper room, perhaps the room they had celebrated Passover in (Mark 14:12–16), to assess the situation.

Luke then tells who was in this initial group. Basically, it is the original twelve (minus Judas Iscariot) and some of the women who so loyally supported Jesus throughout his life and even in his death (John 19:25). In addition to this group, Luke also mentions members of Jesus' family. This last group comes as something of a shock. The family of Jesus did not seem to be amongst his greatest supporters while he was alive, some of them even accusing him of madness (Mark 3:21). Perhaps the death and resurrection of Jesus had caused them to think (and act) differently. Mary seems to have been the only family member to be consistently loyal towards her son.

These three groups form the nucleus of the group which was going to have such a profound impact in the ancient world. It is hard to imagine a less successful bunch of people! Some frightened fishermen and the odd tax collector, supported by a few uneducated women with some only-recently-loyal family members thrown in. Not the best material for launching a new enterprise in a hostile world. Luke lists this unlikely crowd to emphasize that what follows in his book is not the product of human intellect and planning, but is the activity of the risen Jesus, operating by his Spirit. The 'Acts of the Apostles' is the title of the book in the Authorized (King James) translation; another title might be the 'Acts of the Holy Spirit'! There is no mere human explanation for what follows in Luke's story of the early church.

Luke closes this section with a reference to two key principles of success for the first Christians: they were *together* and *in prayer*. United prayer remains an incredibly potent force in any church. Many Christians (and their churches) often substitute activity for prayer when God wants activity as a result of prayer and empowered by prayer. Prayer is the work of the church. It should never be an excuse for idleness or avoiding costly action, but it must precede, accompany and follow all our activity as the people of God.

Replacing a leader (verses 15–26)

Peter, always a man of action, begins a speech designed to encourage the early Christians to choose a successor to Judas Iscariot. It seems that in the days and weeks after the ascension the upper room became a regular meeting place for the committed believers – 120 of them. Peter is emerging as one of the key leaders and immediately points the group back to Scripture as their authority and guide. Judas, whose name is mentioned with anger and disappointment, comes to a gruesome end. He is a traitor, both to Jesus personally and to the first-century believers generally. With the 'blood money' he is given by the Jewish leaders he buys a field in which his own blood is spilled. Peter seems to imply that he gets what he deserves!

If Judas is to be replaced (and Peter quotes Psalms 69:25 and 109:8 to show he ought to be) then they need to establish the personal qualifications required for such a significant task. Peter summarizes the main qualification as being part of the group since Jesus began his ministry – a period of about three years. Their central task would be to act as a witness to the truth of the resurrection. Two candidates emerge. After prayer, they 'cast lots' to see which candidate is successful. Matthias is chosen. In Jewish history, and throughout the ancient world, the throwing of various objects on the ground – dice, stones, bones, etc. – was a common way of discovering the will of God. This was no mere superstition or reliance on 'fate', however. Proverbs 16:33 shows that they believed God was the one who ultimately decided what happened.

This passage identifies three steps in the process of leader selection:

▶ an assessment of personal qualification

▶ commitment of the issue to God in prayer

▶ allowing God to make the appointment.

The first two steps must be undertaken with care and seriousness. There are no short cuts to getting these things right. Individuals who are potential leaders must have their relationship with Jesus examined and every member of the church family must commit the matter to God in prayer. *How* the leader is appointed will vary from church to church (for example by vote; appointment by other leaders; unanimous affirmation, etc.)

depending on our denominational practice or cultural background. Whatever the mechanism for the decision it must allow
God's will to be revealed and acted on.

Questions

1. Make a list of the different ways in which you pray. (You will
   have to decide 'what is prayer?'.) How could you be more
   involved in the prayer-life of your local fellowship?
2. How does your church appoint its leaders? Is it a better or
   worse system than casting lots (verse 26)? Why?
3. Why doesn't everyone who 'betrays' God end up like Judas –
   dead and discredited (verse 18)?

Leadership

Acts records the first leaders of the early church as the apostles.
Because Judas is dead a replacement is needed to keep the
leadership team up to strength (1:20–26). Peter soon emerges as
the dominant personality although the 'chairman' of the
apostolic team seems to be James (15:13; 21:18).

As time goes by elders are appointed (14:23; 15:22) with
responsibility for spiritual oversight for a particular local church
(cf. 20:17). Deacons are appointed in Jerusalem (6:1–6) and
eventually more widely in the local church (cf. Philippians 1:1).
Their role appears to be more specific than the elders, though not
necessarily lower in status. Both groups have high qualification
guidelines (1 Timothy 3:8–13; Titus 1:5–9) but little is known
about their method of appointment or the exact outworking of
their function.

The two other leadership roles appear to be prophet and
teacher (13:1; 21:10; cf. Ephesians 4:11). These roles – apostle,

prophet, elder, deacon, teacher – do not appear to be completely separate ministries; some people seem to exercise more than one role or even a mixture of roles. In Acts the emphasis is not on a definitive description of leadership role or status, but on a statement about gifting and ministry to support a growing church. For the New Testament as a whole function and action, not position or structure, are the important facets of leadership.

Acts 2:1–13

The Holy Spirit is released

All heaven breaks loose at Pentecost as God begins to pour out his spirit on the church.

Pentecost was a well established Jewish feast. It means 'fiftieth' and was a celebration of the grain harvest. Pentecost happened on the fiftieth day after Passover when seven weeks' worth of harvest had been gathered in. It was also the occasion of the anniversary of the law being given on Sinai. The significance of this would not have been lost on the first Christians – the old covenant had been characterized by the operation of the laws, the new covenant would be characterized by the operation of the Spirit. With a marvellous sense of divine timing the new era is ushered in on the anniversary of the old as they meet together.

Luke describes what happens next as best he can considering the incredible event he was witnessing. A noise like a tornado blowing through the room, a roaring fire that appeared from nowhere then separated into individual flames on 120 heads, followed by the expression of lots of different languages being spoken out in wonder and amazement! A scene of godly disorder and holy disarray.

Because it was the feast of Pentecost thousands of Jews found themselves in Jerusalem. They were obviously outside in the street when they heard the commotion among the disciples. Perhaps the noise (followed by the disciples!) burst out of the upper room, developed into a meeting on the streets and ended up as a huge gathering somewhere in the temple precincts. We cannot be sure about the details but we can be certain about the impact on the hearers. They seem to have come from all over the known world and yet they all heard the disciples praising God in their own languages. Even when faced with this amazing miracle some of the crowd thought the whole affair owed its origin to a totally different kind of spirit.

It's important to notice in this passage that, despite the amazing physical signs (noise, fire, tongues), Luke emphasizes the spiritual cause – they 'were filled with the Holy Spirit'. Pentecost is the birth-day of the church. The start of the ministry of Jesus was affirmed by the Spirit (Matthew 3:16) so it is appropriate for the start of the church to be affirmed by the same Spirit.

Questions

1. What do you think it must have felt like to be in Jerusalem on that particular Pentecost? Do you think you would have recognized God at work in all the noise or would you have been on the side of the cynics (verse 13)?

2. Discuss the pros and cons of 'speaking in tongues'. Try to put yourself in the position of a Christian who does not speak in tongues (if you do) or who does (if you don't)! How do you feel? (superior? confident? not bothered?) Share your findings in the group.

3. Why do you think Luke goes to all the trouble of listing so many places by name? Is it significant that 'Arabs' get a mention?

The gift of tongues

The reference in 2:4 to speaking in tongues is the first reference to the phenomenon in Acts. 'Tongues' appears at various points in Luke's account as a sign of the presence of the Holy Spirit (cf. 10:46; 19:6). Luke views it as a common external evidence of the Holy Spirit's activity, but not as an essential manifestation of the filling with the Spirit (e.g., its absence from Paul's conversion story, Acts 9:17–19).

These 'tongues' were human languages on the day of Pentecost, but they appear to be mainly angelic languages in the rest of Acts and the later letters (e.g., 1 Corinthians 13:1). Paul expresses gratitude for the fact that he has this gift (1 Corinthians 14:18) and lays down guidelines for its public use (1 Corinthians 14:5–25).

Paul is critical of the way 'tongues' was used at Corinth, not negative about the gift itself. The Bible seems to give little support to those who wish to consign this gift to history and similarly, little to those who wish to elevate it to an essential requirement of the Spirit-filled life!

Peter explains to the crowd what they have just seen and heard. He describes Pentecost as God keeping his promise to the Jews – a faithful God.

The coming of the Holy Spirit in such a dramatic way certainly got people's attention. Peter is not slow to seize the opportunity to speak to the crowd, trying to explain what has happened. We ought to note the remarkable change in Peter since he denied Jesus (Luke 22:54–61). His restoration by Jesus (John 21:15–22) has transformed him. We can thank God that he does not wash his hands of us when we fail. It's such a large crowd that Peter has to shout to be heard (there is no PA system), and is quick to point out how early in the morning it is. Their behaviour is not the result of alcoholic excess ·but the fulfilment of the prophecy of Joel 2:28–32.

The Jews were looking for the day when Messiah would come, 'the last days', bringing with him great signs of power. This new era would see God's Spirit being released on men and women, young and old . . . with prophecies, dreams and visions being the order of the day. How different this was from the old era, when only specially chosen individuals had access to the Spirit's power. Now he is available to *all people* (verse 17). 'God told Joel about this, Joel passed it on, and what you see here today is simply God doing what he said he would,' Peter informs the astonished gathering.

The details of Joel's prophecy are of little interest to Peter. He does not stop to explain about the blood and fire or the moon turning to blood. These things may have happened on the afternoon of the crucifixion (Luke 23:44–45), they may be symbolic or perhaps they will occur when the Messiah who has just left (1:11) comes back to judge the world (Revelation 6:12). We cannot be certain about these issues and anyway we ought to emphasize the general thrust of the passage as Peter does.

The central message is that God is faithful to what he promises; the Holy Spirit has been released just as Joel prophesied. The new era has begun. And this new era is open to 'everyone who calls on the name of the Lord'. What an amazing offer! And this special offer has never been withdrawn; we can take advantage of it at the end of the twentieth century just as they did at the start of the first century.

The prophecies are fulfilled in Jesus (verses 22–28)

This part of the sermon emphasizes the humanity of Jesus. The word 'man' is used twice in verses 22 and 23 and he is identified as coming from a town many of them would know – about 60 miles north of Jerusalem. But even the crowd knew he was not an ordinary man: some would have eaten with the five thousand (Luke 9:10–17), seen the sick healed (Mark 1:32–34), or heard the amazing reports about Lazarus (John 11:38–48). Despite all this, the crowd was guilty of hounding this extraordinary man to his death, a brutal death by Roman execution. God's hand was in all this to work out his purposes, but that did not excuse their awful behaviour. They killed God's messenger!

Peter, who has only just realized this himself (John 20:3–9), describes the death of Jesus like the birth pains before birth, agonizing and painful, but resulting in life not death. Yet again he quotes the Old Testament (Psalm 16:8–11) to demonstrate that God is doing what he said he would. By calling David as a witness for the prosecution Peter cites one of the great heroes of the Jewish faith. If anyone can convince them of the error of their ways and the truth of what Peter is saying, surely David can! They are guilty as charged.

In his psalm David points, prophetically, to God's care of his Son – he would not be 'abandoned'. Of course, Jesus felt abandoned and utterly alone (Psalm 22:1; cf. Matthew 27:46), but after three days he was wonderfully raised to life. God was faithful to his word, despite what seemed like a lot of evidence to the contrary. Because of the embalming process his body did not even begin to decay over those three days (John 19:39–40). What was written hundreds of years earlier (about 980 BC?) was fulfilled in Jesus!

These verses point us to Jesus, the focal point of God's purpose and plan. As we look to Jesus and the way the Father was faithful to him we can draw strength for ourselves. Many of us have periods in our lives when we feel terribly alone, abandoned by God to fend for ourselves. We may have been abused, bereaved or rejected. Whatever our feelings we can be sure about God's faithfulness. He did not forsake his son, he will not forsake his sons and daughters.

Questions

1. What does 'be saved' (verse 21) mean? Saved from what? Why? How?
2. Do prophecy, visions and dreams have a place in church life today? What are the strengths/dangers of these things?
3. Which groups of people in the world might think that God has abandoned them? How can we help them?

Acts 2:29–36

Pentecost linked with the resurrection

Jesus is divine and has risen from the dead. There is no-one like Jesus!

Peter, by now rising to a crescendo of passion in preaching, points out the obvious. David is dead. So Psalm 16 cannot be about him; it must be about somebody else. And as David has not 'ascended' into heaven, Psalm 110:1 can't be about him either (cf. verses 34–35). Jesus had already implied that this psalm was about himself (Mark 12:35–37) and Peter builds on this understanding. Notice again the emphasis on the reliability and faithfulness of God: he 'promised him on oath' and God was as good as his word.

The resurrection of Jesus is the central fact of this sermon; everything else hangs on this truth. Peter is at pains to point out that he is not guessing about this or going on rumour or second-hand reports. He saw Jesus alive from the dead with his own eyes (1 Corinthians 15:5) and so had these other disciples standing with him (1:3; cf. verse 32; 1 Corinthians 15:6). There is no doubt about it. Peter's implication is that this fact is beyond dispute. They (like us!) could debate, procrastinate or even deny it, but nothing would change the truth.

What must have really shocked this already 'amazed' congregation was what Peter said about the alive Jesus. Firstly, he told them that Jesus was none other than the Messiah they had been looking for – the Christ. The Messiah (Christ is the Greek word for Messiah: 'The anointed one') was Jesus. They need look for him no longer.

Secondly, Jesus was the Lord. Old Testament prophecies about

God are taken as applying to Jesus; Peter is putting Jesus on the same level as God himself! This revelation must have been staggering to the gathered Jewish crowd. All the honour, adoration and worship which they had reserved for God alone was also due to a poor carpenter from Nazareth.

The early disciples were clear about who Jesus was. They would have found many of our explanations of Jesus quite funny in a tragic sort of way. 'Just a good man', 'a wise teacher', 'an example of love and kindness' . . . all these accolades fall far short of Peter's clear, full-blooded, uncompromising description of the One who ushered in God's kingdom (1:3). He is the 'anointed one', fully God and fully man. The defeater of death and the baptizer with the Holy Spirit!

Questions

1. None of us saw the resurrection of Jesus with our own eyes. In what ways can we testify that it is true? In our experience? Intellectually?
2. 'Jesus was just a good man.' What reasons would you give for disagreeing with this statement?
3. Peter really emphasizes the resurrection. Why do you think it is such an important part of Christian faith? What would happen to Christianity if it wasn't true (see 1 Corinthians 15:14)?

Prophecy

Prophets in the New Testament had a ministry inspired by the Spirit of foretelling future events (11:28; 21:10–11) and of building up the people of God (15:32; 1 Corinthians 14:3). Sometimes they had a travelling ministry (11:27) and on other

39

occasions seemed to be attached to a specific local situation, for example, Antioch (13:1).

The *gift* of prophecy could also be exercised by those who were not necessarily called to the *ministry* of the prophet (2:17–18; 19:6), so 'ordinary' Christians could use this gift to build up the church. Paul values the gift very highly indeed (1 Corinthians 14:5) and encourages its use in the church (1 Corinthians 14:1).

Acts 2:37–47

The growing church

There is an amazing response to Peter's sermon and the church begins to get established. Being Christian soon affects every part of their lives.

Many in the crowd were convicted by the thought that they had contributed to the death of God's Messiah. Their spirits were in great distress, 'cut to the heart', as they pleaded with Peter about what to do. Peter immediately offers a two-step solution:

- *repentance*, a complete change of mind, turning around and going the other way;

- *baptism*, acknowledging that Jesus really is God's Anointed One.

When they do this all their evil will be forgiven and they too will receive the blessing of the new era – the Holy Spirit. And the offer is not restricted to them but available to family and friends, even to those who lived many miles away from Jerusalem.

Immediately 3,000 people responded to this offer (the original 'upper room' group is increased 25 times over in one day!) and joined themselves to the believers. This led to the rapid introduction of a discipleship course which covered such foundational subjects as Christian doctrine, fellowship, communion and prayer. Just as in the first century, it is a vitally important part of church life to provide for the nurture and care of new converts.

The passage goes on to describe life in the early church. The church was characterized by signs of

- supernatural power (verse 43)

- prolonged fellowship (verse 44)

- generous and sacrificial giving (verse 45)

- eating and praising God (verses 46–47)

- meeting on a daily basis (verse 46), no doubt for worship and teaching.

As the early Christians multiplied and spread out over the ancient world some of the details in this pattern changed, but the principles were retained. It was not Luke's intention to imply, for example, that Christians must meet together every day as they did here, but it is obviously his intention to highlight the value of regular gatherings for prayer, fellowship and worship. Churches must be very careful as they apply this passage to congregational life. We may feel justified in reducing 'everything in common' to 'sharing a few things', and 'selling their possessions' to 'trying to be generous', but we ought to note that we have also managed to reduce 'wonders and miraculous signs' to 'no-one was converted but God really blessed us'!

Such was the power of God on these believers that *every day* new people were joining the worshipping community. What a thrill to be part of a church like this!

Questions

---

1. What signs are there in a person's life when repentance is real?
2. What do we need to do to make sure new Christians keep growing and are kept from drifting away?
3. Why do we find sharing our possessions so difficult? What do you think a first-century Christian would think of the way we treat the things we own?

Prayer

Prayer was a vital part of the life of the early church. It was a significant part of their spiritual lives together (2:42) and a major part of the apostles' role (6:4) as leaders in the Christian community. They prayed for protection and boldness (4:24–30)

▶ when ordaining elders, deacons and missionaries (18:23; 6:6; 13:3);

▶ when wanting to help people receive the Holy Spirit (8:15);

▶ as a regular exercise of corporate worship (3:1; 16:13).

They offered prayers of praise (4:24), thanksgiving (27:35) and desperation (12:5)! They saw prayer as part and parcel of their corporate walk with God. There is very little emphasis on personal prayer in Acts. A fleeting reference to Peter (10:9) and Paul (9:11) praying privately is the only mention it gets!

Praying with other Christians is highlighted as the mechanism God uses

▶ to reveal his will

▶ to release his blessing and

▶ to accomplish his purposes.

Acts 3:1–10

The first healing

God acts in power to confirm the ministry of the apostles and the authority of his Son. It is a miracle motivated by compassion.

Peter and John were going to pray, along with other Jews, at the temple. This was the second of three prayer opportunities each day (early morning, mid-afternoon and sun-set) which the Jews observed. They see a chronically disabled beggar on his way to the temple, not to pray but to beg. This was not an unusual sight in ancient Jerusalem; Peter and John must have passed dozens of pathetic characters on their journey to prayer. For some reason they are drawn to this particular beggar and they lead him to believe that he is in for a sizeable donation when they command him to 'look at us'. His hopes are dashed as Peter tells the man of his own poverty: presumably he had given everything away (2:45). His hopes are revived by a mind-blowing statement which draws on the power of Jesus and results in a clear command – 'walk'.

It is important to note that Peter is not responsible for the healing – Jesus is. Peter is the agent God uses (and his courage in making this statement ought to be applauded), but the power for the healing comes from the Anointed One, better known to the people in Jerusalem as Jesus from Nazareth.

The beggar cannot believe his ears and needs Peter to offer the 'right hand of fellowship' to encourage him to his feet. He is completely and instantaneously healed! And this is a man who has never, ever walked before. He was born with a body deformed in some way, giving him a 'permanent' disability. No wonder he cannot keep still. He leaps and jumps and walks . . . and all the time is praising God. The temple courts had never seen anything like it. People were 'filled with wonder' at this man they may just have given some money to as a disabled beggar, now rushing about all over the place celebrating his healing by worshipping God.

It is particularly thrilling that the first miracle of the early church recorded in detail, should be such a difficult one. You might have expected the apostles to start by trying to heal someone with a cold, a sprained ankle or a small boil! No, they jump straight in at the deep end, with a man who has been crippled from birth. Nothing is too difficult for Jesus. As Peter and John discovered, the 'impossible' is possible for him.

Questions

1. Does the 'name of Jesus' (verse 6b) still have the same power to heal today? In what ways should we encourage this?
2. Peter and John had no money (verse 6a) but they were used to heal this sick man. Do you think there is a connection between these two (i.e., poverty and power)? How does it apply to us today?
3. This miracle is both quick and complete. Why do you think that healing like this is so rare today? Is God somehow restricted?

Miracles

There are at least eighteen specific supernatural events recorded in Acts and another ten occasions where there is a general reference to miracles occurring. This is an average of one reference for each of the 28 chapters in Acts. It is impossible to remove them from the story without destroying the account completely. Luke does not record these miracles with exaggeration or dwell on them excessively; they simply form one part of the life of the early church, so he reports them accurately and concisely.

It is hardly surprising that a God who can raise Jesus from the dead is capable of other (easier?) miracles. These supernatural events seem to occur most when the gospel is proclaimed for the first time in a particular location or to a particular group. They seem to be performed mainly by the leadership of the church. In combination with teaching (cf. 13:9–12) they result in thousands discovering Jesus.

Acts 3:11-26

The healing points to Jesus

**Peter takes the opportunity of the healing
miracle to preach an evangelistic message.**

Faith in the name of Jesus
(verses 11–16)

This healed beggar will not let Peter and John
out of his sight. Perhaps he thinks once they go, his healing
would also go (an understandable fear, but he is mistaken). He
'held on to' the apostles – it is the same phrase used to describe
an arrest by the police – clinging to them while the crowd grows
around the unlikely trio. Fortunately, Solomon's colonnade was
large, running the entire length of the eastern end of the temple.
Once the crowd assemble Peter, never one to miss an opportunity, preaches a sermon of explanation. It has a number of the
same elements as the Pentecost sermon:

- the opening style (verse 12; cf. 2:22)

- an accusation about killing Jesus (verses 13–15; cf. 2:23)

- the exaltation by God of Jesus (verse 13; cf. 2:36)

- Peter's own credentials as a witness of the resurrection
  (verse 15; cf. 2:32).

If anything, this sermon is even more passionate in tone than
the Pentecost sermon. Verses 13b–15a contain a damning
indictment of the Jews, a blunt, accusatory attack on their role
in the death of Jesus. Peter makes no attempt to soften these

savage verbal blows – this is no-nonsense preaching at its most direct. We have much to learn from this. Gentleness and discretion are important facets of the preacher's skill, but this must never be allowed to blunt the cutting edge of the message. We are often far too afraid of causing offence or upsetting people with a raw, unpackaged presentation of gospel truth. We must pray for a holy boldness.

Peter is at pains to refuse all credit for the miracle and points to both a divine aspect and a human aspect in the cure. It is the name of Jesus which has power (cf. 2:38) and the power is seen in response to faith. In this case it is the faith of Peter and John, not the faith of the crippled man. And there is no possibility of a hoax: they had all passed this man, in his disabled condition, day after day as he sat begging at the ornate gateway into the temple area. The crowd themselves were the best evidence for this miracle. There is no escape from the truth about the person of Jesus, nor from the fact of the healing miracle. God has been at work.

A call to repentance (verses 17–26)

The sermon continues, but in more restrained style. They represent the 'carrot' approach, the 'stick' having been effectively used in verses 13–15. Peter addresses them as 'brothers' and concedes that they may not have been completely aware of the implications of what they were doing when they killed Jesus. Ignorance is no excuse (cf. Leviticus 5:17) but it does in some measure lessen their guilt. God had it in mind all along to use the suffering of Christ to accomplish his purposes (verse 18; cf. 2:23).

These verses pose a problem for us in a way that would not have worried the first hearers. We find it hard to reconcile the fact that the death of Jesus was part of God's plan with the fact that he was killed by evil men. How could they be blamed for doing what God had decided to do anyway? The Jews had an understanding of God which allowed him total authority, while giving his creatures the dignity of making meaningful decisions.

47

We are not puppets, being made to respond every time our strings are pulled. The Scripture affirms both truths equally – sinful human beings and the plan of God put Jesus on the cross.

Peter then points the crowd back to their Old Testament Scriptures. These Scriptures have been paving the way for all that they have witnessed in recent weeks. Moses, Samuel, Abraham and 'all the prophets' are quoted as 'signposts' which pointed forward to Jesus. 'These great Jewish leaders foretold the coming of the Messiah and you are immensely privileged, because he has come to you first,' Peter told them.

Repentance is the key to unlocking the blessing of the Christ (cf. 2:38). If they repent there will be implications for the past and the present, continuing on into the future. God will take his sponge and clean out all the dirt from our cuts and wounds ('sins may be wiped out') and into the barren deserts of our lives his presence will come like showers of rain on an oppressively hot day ('times of refreshing'). Repentance is still the key to unlocking the blessings of God. Without genuine repentance we will not experience all that God has for us. The powerlessness of some churchgoers is directly related to the absence of genuine repentance.

Questions

1. In what ways is repentance more than simply 'being sorry'?
2. How many titles or descriptions of God's Son can you find in this passage? What do they mean?
3. Jesus came to the Jews first. Do we have a responsibility to continue to evangelize the Jews? Why have Jews and Christians had a history of distrust?

Becoming a Christian

The book of Acts records several incidents where individuals become Christians, for example, Saul, Cornelius, Lydia, the Philippian jailer, and on numerous occasions records large numbers of people responding to the Good News (e.g., 2:41; 4:4; 14:1; 17:4). We also have excerpts from sermons which call for people to respond to Christ. These three pieces of evidence combine to show us what Luke (and the early church) thought was involved in becoming a follower of Jesus.

There seem to be four aspects to the initial phase of following Jesus:

▶ *Repentance* – a complete turning around and returning to God (2:38; 26:20)

▶ *Belief / faith* – putting trust in the name and power of Jesus (16:31; 20:21)

▶ Baptism in water (8:38; 9:18; 16:15)

▶ The Holy Spirit's power (9:17; 10:44; 19:5).

Sometimes, one or more of these aspects is implied rather than clearly stated, and the order in which they occur varies from case to case. Nevertheless, Luke clearly sees these four things as vital components of the conversion experience. Today we are in danger of emphasizing some of these things to the near exclusion of one or more of the others. It is no wonder that so many Christians do not get the best start to their lives as believers!

Acts 4:1–12

Peter and John on trial

Arrest, imprisonment and trial provide an opportunity to tell about the power of Jesus.

Before Peter's sermon can come to a proper conclusion the chief of security at the temple arrives to see what all the fuss is about. The Sadducees were wealthy aristocrats who had maintained their status and affluence by collaborating with the Roman authorities. A disturbance in the temple is the last thing they need if relationships with the Romans are to be kept sweet. Not only that, Peter's message is all about resurrection which they did not believe in: all in all, two good reasons for hushing the whole thing up and having the apostles thrown in prison.

Jesus had warned his disciples to expect persecution (Luke 21:12); perhaps they had not thought it would come quite this quickly! Despite the apostles being hauled away in mid-sentence, however, many people were convinced and joined the church. There are now over forty times as many believers as there were on the day of Pentecost (1:15; cf. verse 4).

The Jewish council is convened – Luke is at pains to point out that the top people are there – this is obviously a serious matter. They demand to know what is going on. Peter, pentecostally empowered, speaks for both the apostles when he gives a robust defence of their actions. Jesus had promised they would have special power in situations like this (Luke 12:11–12) and so it proved.

Peter makes the point that they ought to be pleased that a sick man is now well – after all, it was an 'act of kindness'. They had not healed the crippled man, Jesus had. The Jewish rulers were guilty of doing away with the Christ, in fulfilment of Psalm 118:22. If they wanted to be forgiven for this sin in particular and other sins in general they could find salvation in Jesus and nowhere else. This is not a speech designed to win friends!

Verse 12 is the clearest statement so far in Acts of the uniqueness of Jesus. It has been implied by the disciples (John 6:68) and stated by Jesus (John 14:6). Now it appears in the teaching and experience of the early church. It carries with it a blunt denial of the ability of the Jewish law (or any Roman or Greek deity that was popular at the time) to effect salvation. In a world of many faiths and religious viewpoints Christianity continues to need this emphasis. Humbly communicated, it can energize our evangelism and enrich our worship.

Questions

1. 'All religions lead to God.' How does verse 12 affect our response to this claim?
2. How many 'acts of kindness' (verse 9) have you done today? How can your house group/church develop a practical ministry of 'kindness'?
3. Very few of us have been imprisoned for our faith. How can we support those who are persecuted for their faith around the world?

Sanhedrin

The Sanhedrin was the highest authority in Jewish affairs. It was patterned on the court of Moses (Numbers 11:16–17) and had 70 members and a presiding chairman who co-ordinated its activities. Membership was only possible for Jewish married men who were over 30 years old.

There were three groups represented on the Sanhedrin:

▶ *Rulers* – chief priests and priests with an official role or status in the synagogue;

▶ *Elders* – those in lay-leadership who were often drawn from wealthy aristocratic families;

▶ *Scribes* – legal experts, often Pharisees.

Together, this group formed the supreme council among the Jews. In the past it had enjoyed a good reputation but by the time of Jesus was dominated by self-serving 'politicians', not the godly men originally in mind when the council was formed. The New Testament views it almost always in a negative light:

▶ it was threatened by Jesus' ministry (John 11:47–53);

▶ it engineered his death (Matthew 26:59);

▶ it attempted to bully his church into silence (Acts 5:21–40).

Sadducees

The Sadducees were a political group with considerable influence at the time of Jesus and the early church. They were not a large group numerically (many fewer than the Pharisees) but were made up of wealthy, influential individuals. They were very close to the Roman administration, often collaborating with the occupying power and were not above bribery (or threats) to maintain their positions of power.

They did not believe in the resurrection and on this point found themselves opposed by both the Pharisees and the

Christians (Acts 23:6–8). Two of the three groups on the Sanhedrin (elders and rulers) would tend to support the Sadducees party.

Pharisees

The Pharisees were a large group of men who were character-ized by their commitment to the customs and traditions of Judaism. They often had legal training and were sticklers for obedience to every single part of Jewish law. During the ministry of Jesus they regularly opposed him and his message (e.g., Luke 5:21–30). Jesus reserved some of his strongest language for this group (e.g., Luke 11:39f).

By the time of the early church, however, their stance against the Christians had softened. The Pharisee, Gamaliel, comes to the Christians' rescue (Acts 5:34); they side with the Christians (against the Sadducees) about 'resurrection' (Acts 23:8); and some of their number even become Christians (Acts 15:5). Their most famous convert is the Apostle Paul (Acts 23:6).

Acts 4:13–22

Warned but set free

The trial ends with the apostles being released but warned about future behaviour. Their faith is undiminished by the Sanhedrin's threats.

The Jewish ruling council is amazed by the boldness of the fishermen. By background they are the opposite of those who make up the Council. Peter and John had no profes-sional or academic qualifications and yet could articulate their views with amazing clarity. Jesus had obviously taught them well.

The Council found itself in a difficult position. The man was obviously healed after over 40 years of disability and his presence at the trial made dismissing this evidence difficult. The crowd was delighted at God's healing power; everyone in the city was aware of the incredible thing Peter and John had done the day before and hundreds had decided to follow Jesus. The Sanhedrin could only threaten them with punishment in the future if they kept on talking about Jesus. They were desperate for 'peace at any price'. Civic disturbances would attract the attention of the Roman authorities and put at risk their positions of power and influence.

The apostles and the Sanhedrin behave in ways which act as an example – one positive, the other negative! What matters to God is not our academic or intellectual ability but our openness to him. Peter and John should have been 'taken to the cleaners' by the professors on the Sanhedrin. This would not be the last time God would demonstrate his power through the underdog (1 Corinthians 1:26–31). And notice how the Sanhedrin (all religious leaders) do not even discuss whether or not what Peter says is *true*; their minds are closed. Protecting their vested interests is all that concerns them. May God give us the courage always to be open to the truth – even if it challenges our lifestyle and behaviour.

Peter and John refuse to be cowed into silence. 'Make your own mind up,' they say, 'should we obey you or God?' This is not rebellion against authority for its own sake, but rather the only possible response to an edict which was directly opposed to what Jesus had told them to do (Matthew 28:18–20; Acts 1:8). Not only that, they just cannot help themselves! The sight of the risen Jesus and all he taught them just can't be kept quiet. They *have* to let the Good News out.

Questions

1. Why are we so frightened about what people will think of us or say about us? How can we overcome this?
2. Do you need a degree or professional qualification to be a leader in your church? What qualifications are important for leaders (e.g., look at verses 8, 13b, 19)?
3. Is our definition of a good sermon, 'one we agree with'? Why is this dangerous? What are the characteristics of a closed mind?

Persecution

Luke tells an exciting story of life and growth as he describes the early church. But it is also a story of pain, pressure and persecution. The success of the first Christians was not without considerable cost.

They had recently lost their leader (1:9) and were soon being imprisoned (4.3); threatened (4:21); imprisoned again (5:18); and cruelly flogged (5:40). Stephen was stoned by a lynch-mob (7:57–58); James, the brother of John, was beheaded (12:2); and Paul was (amongst other things!) stoned (14:19), severely beaten (16:22–23), imprisoned (16:24) . . . and shipwrecked (27:39–44)!

Let no-one doubt the incredible cost of Christian discipleship. These first-century believers certainly paid the price for their allegiance to Jesus. We may envy the success recorded in Acts, but we often forget the sacrifice that accompanied it.

Acts 4:23–37

The praying and sharing church

Peter and John join their friends for prayer. Worship and intercession lead to a fresh touch from God, which results in ever bolder evangelism.

Prayer and worship (verses 23–31)

After the council releases them the dynamic duo report back to their fellow believers. As they recount the incident, the early church feels two conflicting emotions: *joy* because of the healing miracle and *frustration*, with a little fear, at the response of the Sanhedrin. These two responses dictate the shape of their prayer – *praise* and *thanksgiving* (verses 24–28), followed by *petition* (verses 29–30).

Notice that prayer is their first response to the crisis (an example we would do well to emulate!) and it is a prayer that has God as its focus from the start. When in doubt start by reminding yourself how great God is. This prayer talks of his supreme status as ruler over all he has created. Psalm 2 is quoted as a reminder of the futility of trying to thwart God's purposes, then the prayer goes on to affirm the controlling hand of God over all that has happened. The message of the first part of the prayer is – God is in charge. When trouble comes into our lives we would do well to remind ourselves of these characteristics of our God. They are designed to bring comfort and reassurance, just as they did here in the first century.

The prayer continues with a request for three things. They weren't:

■▶ get the Sanhedrin off our backs

■▶ give us an alternative strategy

■▶ please grant us a quiet life.

These prayers would certainly feature in many of our churches if we were faced with this situation!

They asked for:

■▶ God to take note of who his enemies were ('consider their threats')

■▶ an increased boldness in speaking the word and

■▶ evidence of the supernatural.

God was well aware of the trouble the religious leaders would cause the early church; his Son had not found them helpful, neither would his followers (Matthew 10:17, 24; 16:12; 26:59). The other two requests were answered in a spectacular and decisive fashion. The place where they were meeting was shaken (a divinely timed earthquake?) and the following days saw their courage increase.

Luke tells us that they were again filled with the Holy Spirit.

57

The outward signs are different from the filling they received at Pentecost (2:2–4), but the experience is no less real. We should look for signs of God's Spirit in those who claim to be filled with him; but the nature of the sign must not absorb our attention, distracting us from the necessity of the filling!

Practical acts of compassion (verses 32–37)

There is no doubt that the early church saw the sharing of possessions as a significant expression of their faith (cf. 2:44). Luke believes these expressions of social concern are the outworking of the spiritual reality of the filling with the Holy Spirit. Just as tongues (2:4) and boldness (verse 31) are 'natural' results of the Spirit's activity, so Luke infers that loving, selfless sharing is another characteristic of the Spirit-filled life. And it all flows from a unity of spirit and purpose which creates an atmosphere in which generosity can flourish.

The passage then reminds us that the foundation for all this is the *resurrection*. It is the pivotal truth on which everything rests. Without the resurrection there would have been no Pentecost, no Spirit-filling, no bold proclamation of the gospel and no sharing lifestyle. As long as they keep on emphasizing the resurrection God's favour will be with them.

Such was the power of love in this close-knit community that abject poverty, common in the ancient world, was unknown among them (cf. Deuteronomy 15:4). It was not that nobody owned anything, but that they treated possessions so lightly as to be willing to give them up when a need became apparent. You cannot sell things 'from time to time' if you do not own them! Some political and religious groups have tried to see in the early chapters of Acts a pattern for communal living which treats all property and wealth as owned by the group as a whole, not by individuals within it. A careful reading of the passage rejects this conclusion. Nevertheless, community living, where carefully established and led, does provide an excellent opportunity for expressing the teaching of this passage. Most 'average' church life runs the opposite risk – an overly protective attitude to personal possessions, which expresses itself in a narrow view of 'fellowship' and a lack of generosity.

To illustrate this sacrificial sharing, Luke introduces us to Barnabas. He is an encourager by name and by nature. 'At the apostles' feet' is a phrase used to stress that this is an offering to God, placed at the disposal of the leadership, for the good of all the believers. There is no compulsion here; Barnabas gives in response to need, motivated by compassion.

Questions

1. Jesus told the 'rich young man' to sell everything he had (Mark 10:21). Does this passage teach that every Christian should do the same? How can we apply the lessons of these verses to our lives today?
2. What amount from your church funds is spent on the poor – here and overseas? How can the poor be helped by the church family?
3. List some governments or organizations, at home and overseas, which threaten the church. How can we support those Christians who are most at risk?

Acts 5:1–16

A disaster and a healing

**Two individuals conspire together to deceive
the apostles. God is not fooled! They pay
a terrible price for their sinful action.**

A warning to others (verses 1–11)

Ananias and Sapphira, perhaps seeing the
high esteem in which Barnabas was held,
decided to bring an offering to the apostles. They sold a piece of
real estate to make a monetary gift possible. What follows is a
sad story of human failing and folly. They agree between them
that the money is too much to give away so they will give a
proportion of it to the church, but then claim that it is the total
amount received for the property they sold. Peter helps them
(and us) to see that the sin is *not* giving less than the full amount,
but pretending it *is* the full amount. Bringing a smaller offering
than they *could* is not wrong; bringing a smaller offering than
they *claimed* they were giving is (verse 4).

Ananias is struck dead. Perhaps he had a heart attack at the
shock of being found out. If he did Luke would see this as a
secondary cause. For the writer of Acts the primary cause of his
death is clear – the judgment of God (cf. 12:23). Sapphira then
comes in and is given a chance by Peter to tell the truth. She
responds with a blatant lie. She too is struck dead and is buried
with her husband, ending her life just three hours after he has
ended his. We hardly need to be told by Luke that this incident
generated 'fear' among the believers and in the wider community.

To modern minds this story comes as something of a shock.
Part of this lies in our failure to understand the seriousness of the

situation which Luke records. Peter saw two people, motivated by envy of Barnabas (and others), manipulating God's people for their own ends; they had lied to God and attempted to deceive the apostles. This betrayal of trust could not go unchallenged. If it had the new Christian movement could have been derailed in the first stages of its journey. Deceit of this kind would poison relationships, compromise the Christian community and reduce the thrust of its witness. A decisive act is called for. (This passage has parallels with Joshua 7:1–26, where Achan is dealt with in a similarly decisive manner.)

The word 'church' is used for the first time here in Acts. A 'mixed-bag' group of believers from many backgrounds and age groups is being welded together as the 'church'. If the new-born church is not to be the still-born church tough action is necessary against sin of this kind.

Good news spreads (verses 12–16)

Luke reminds us in this passage that despite the threats from the Sanhedrin (4:18, 21) and the pressures of internal pastoral problems (e.g., verses 1–11), the church continues to be extremely active. Incredible miracles and supernatural signs of God's activity are the order of the day. It's interesting that Luke thinks of the apostles as the primary agents of the miraculous, rather than individual believers from the rank-and-file of the church (cf. 2:43; 4:33) and the major healing incidents recorded all involve the leadership. Every believer had a common purpose and commitment (4:32), each one was filled with the Spirit (2:4; 4:31), all met for worship and prayer (verse 12b; cf. 2:46) but apparently only a small group of leaders regularly ministered in this specific 'signs and wonders' way.

Solomon's Colonnade was becoming a regular gathering place for Christians (cf. 3:11). They were held in great esteem by the general public, and the church continued to experience significant numerical growth. Nevertheless, mixed in with the great esteem was a large portion of fear. You would be wise to avoid that eastern Colonnade if you did not want to be associated with those Christians. The Council had made their views extremely clear and were very influential. Associating with Christians might cost you promotion at work, status in the community . . . or worse! Perhaps people started to come to the temple through the western gate, just to be on the safe side. And the incident with Ananias and Sapphira hadn't helped – 'Have you heard about the way they treat you if you step out of line?' – no wonder people were afraid!

But good news spreads, and such is the desperate state of many of the sick and demonized that they come to the Christians despite the risks. Luke is struck by the fact that the apostles are simply carrying on where Jesus left off. Verse 16 sounds amazingly like Luke 4:37, 40. By the power of the Holy Spirit they are continuing the ministry of their Master. All this excitement does seem to have generated some hero-worship of Peter and a somewhat 'magical' view of his healing prowess. It's easy for us to ridicule their primitive and superstitious actions but we should take care. God seems to honour their faith in him, however naively or crudely it may be expressed. He had healed in similar circumstances in the past (Jesus in Mark 5:28–29) and would do so again in the future (Paul in Acts 19:11–12).

Questions

1. Should we expect healing miracles today? Through our leaders? Any Christian? Where does modern medicine fit in?
2. Peter exercised severe church discipline. Should church discipline be used more than it is today? Or less? Under what circumstances?
3. Some people avoided the early church out of fear. People tend to avoid the church today through boredom or irrelevance. What do you think of this change?

Acts 5:17–42

The authorities pile on the pressure

**Ever-increasing 'official' pressure
fails to stifle evangelistic zeal.**

Arrest and escape (verses 17–20)

Motivated by envy at the apostles' standing with the people, the Sadducees have the Christian leadership rounded up and thrown in jail with the common thieves and criminals. A night in a prison with characters like these was not an attractive prospect. No doubt the high priest and his cronies were hoping that some mental and physical abuse would soften the apostles up a bit for the next day's hearing! But God had other ideas – a jail-break was arranged, courtesy of an angel. The angel instructed them to go back to the temple precinct area and tell the people the good news, not missing anything out (note the phrase 'full message' in verse 20). They are not to tone things down or leave out the controversial bits – despite the pressure and harassment.

The directive of the angel is outrageously audacious, but they do it. So much of this account in the early chapters of Acts contrasts with church life today. They were bold, direct, rude and produced a commotion wherever they went. We are often timid, evasive, overly polite and produce a stifled yawn wherever we go! This description may be a caricature, but an honest assessment of our church life and theirs could not miss the obvious contrast between us.

Arrested again (verses 21–26)

While the apostles are back in the temple court preaching the
security guards are at the prison to bring them to the hearing.
This section is not without its humorous side. It has many of the
ingredients of a TV situation comedy. The security guards are
confused (no obvious sign of a break out), the chief priests
'puzzled' and everyone on the Sanhedrin, that august and
important group, is embarrassed and wondering how you can
have a hearing when there is no-one to hear. There is a lot of egg
on a lot of faces! Finally the riddle of the missing apostles is
solved: an ordinary worshipper has seen them on his way to
prayer – they are preaching again. At this news the chief of
security and his men go to bring the apostles to the Council.
They are gentle and respectful because of the apostles' popularity.

Much of this echoes the ministry of Jesus, who was often in
trouble with the authorities but was followed enthusiastically by
the ordinary people (Mark 12:37).

Another trial (verses 27–33)

After the fiasco of the night before the Sanhedrin is in no mood
for tolerance. They are desperate to hush this whole thing up
before the Romans get wind of it and they are faced with a
rebellious group of people who have totally ignored the last
court order (4:16; cf. 5:12, 21). In addition, they may have begun
to feel the weight of the accusations about their responsibility for
the death of Jesus (cf. 4:10). Their reputation as a Council would
be damaged if they had 'rigged' the death of an innocent man,
and if that man was even suspected of being the Messiah . . . the
implications for their positions and status were too awful to
contemplate.

Peter (with the occasional 'hear, hear' from the others) merely
restates his position (cf. 4:19). They are only doing what God has
told them. Once on his feet, Peter treats the Council to another

potted sermon, repeating the basic facts of their message. Some of the Sanhedrin have heard this talk before! 'Jesus is more than an ordinary man (cf. 2:36; 4:12), you are guilty of killing him (cf. 2:36; 4:10), and we have seen him alive' (cf. 2:32; 4:33).

The Council are livid, beside themselves with rage – just as they had been with Jesus (Matthew 26:65). How dare Peter speak to them in this way! His statement implies that they are opposing God, have missed out on recognizing the Messiah (even though they were looking for him), killed the Messiah; are obstructing his work and will not get all God's blessing (the Holy Spirit) until they stop being disobedient and start obeying God. And all this delivered by a Galilean nobody who was more at home with fish than theologians! No wonder they were angry enough to want the apostles killed.

This passage contrasts two groups of leaders. The apostles had genuine integrity; they did not encourage their followers to do one thing and do another themselves. These were not generals who hid behind their troops. They faced threats, harassment, imprisonment, flogging, even death. No wonder their leadership was respected and followed. By contrast the Sanhedrin had collaborated and compromised with the Romans at every level. Ordinary Jews suffered while they retained their privileges. They had legal 'clout' but no moral authority to rule; they were leaders who had lost the right to lead.

Gamaliel to the rescue (verses 34–42)

The Council may have wanted to put the apostles to death but they did not have the power to do so. Only the occupying power of Rome could sanction the death penalty. They would have to concoct some kind of charge, as they did with Jesus, to convince the Romans that a death sentence was appropriate. They were deflected from this course of action by one of the most respected religious leaders of the day, a Pharisee named Gamaliel. The Pharisees were less influential on the Council than the Sadducees but were still a significant part of the power structure. Gamaliel was widely honoured as an outstanding expert on the law, and a man of high moral character and religious fervour. Presumably he had witnessed the excessive ravings of the Sadducees with some distaste and decided to speak his mind before anything rash was done.

Gamaliel had the defendants removed so he could speak his mind more easily. He argued that these revolutionary movements come and go. Had not Theudas been seen as a great threat? Now he was dead and the whole thing had blown over; exactly the same had happened to Judas the Galilean. 'Don't over-react,' he warns them, 'It will all fizzle out.' And he goes on to argue that if it does not, it will be God's will that it succeeds, so you had better not try to oppose God.

It is important not to read too much into the speech. Gamaliel is not on the verge of converting to Christianity. The Pharisees were closer to the apostles theologically than the Sadducees (for example, the Pharisees had a belief in the resurrection) and were less politically compromised. They were religious experts and teachers, often quite poor, and with a reputation for a strict commitment to every detail of the law. They had an overwhelming belief in the will of God (a kind of 'if it happens it must be God's will' mentality) which gave them quite a fatalistic approach to things. Gamaliel's closing words sound very like Peter's but the resemblance is superficial. He presents his whole case from the Pharisees' point of view. The Sadducees may not have been persuaded by the logic of Gamaliel's arguments, but they could see the sense in not over-reacting. They had the apostles flogged (39 lashes perhaps, see Deuteronomy 25:3), re-issued the court order to be silent, and released them.

The apostles feel privileged to be allowed to suffer for their Lord and completely ignore the court order! The trial and punishment has the opposite effect from what it was supposed to.

Questions

1. Would you have obeyed the Sanhedrin and kept quiet (verse 28)? Can you think of times when you ought to obey God rather than human authority?
2. Why was the early church different from the church today? Should we try to change? If so, how?
3. Persecution often stimulates faith. Imagine that you head an anti-Christian regime. How would you stamp out the church? What can Christians learn from this?

Acts 6:1–15
Practical service

The apostles initiate a practical solution to a pastoral problem. Needs are met, new workers are commissioned and the church keeps on growing.

Spiritual pastoral care (verses 1–7)

The chapter begins with a reminder that in the early church things do not stand still – numerical growth continues unabated. This is the fifth specific reference to increase in numbers in these early chapters of Acts; for Luke it's the natural result of a clear presentation of the gospel in the power of the Holy Spirit. He adds a sixth reference (verse 7) and excitedly points out that even the priests are turning to Christ in sizeable numbers. For this infant movement to be making inroads into the Establishment is a sign of its power and growing influence. God is on the move!

But the church has an internal pastoral problem to solve. Widows, who had no other means of provision, were cared for from a common purse. However, Jews who spoke mainly Greek (and may well have moved to Jerusalem from another country, leaving themselves cut off from family support) felt that in comparison to the local-born widows they were getting a bit of a raw deal. We are not told how this happened but the apostles (here given their technical title – 'the twelve') are concerned to put it right, although not at any cost. They must retain their ministry of communicating God's word if the church is to remain healthy.

Spreading the work-load

The apostles also refuse to impose a solution but suggest, to the whole group, that they appoint seven more workers to spread the work-load. These men must have had an encounter with God and be wise administrators. Note that both *spiritual* and *practical* qualifications are required. Many a church has appointed a skilled accountant as treasurer but regretted it because of an absence of spirituality! The group agrees with this idea and promptly chooses seven men to ensure that all the different groups in the early church are represented fairly. The seven are then commissioned by the apostles by the laying on of hands (cf. Numbers 27:23) – a visual aid of the process of giving authority to this group to serve. The group are never described as deacons by Luke, but do seem to exercise a parallel ministry to that described by Paul in 1 Timothy 3:8–13.

The early Christians were learning what the children of Israel had had to learn about leadership – delegate or die (cf. Exodus 18)! More people had to be involved in all the different aspects of ministry and leadership if the church was to continue growing.

Stephen's ministry takes off (verses 8–15)

We are not entirely sure why Stephen has such an impact in his ministry of communicating truth and power when he is supposed to be waiting on tables! Certainly only the apostles have been credited with such amazing power up to this point; they seem to have passed this authority on to Stephen when he was commissioned for ministry. It is a clear reminder to us that God is sovereign and perfectly capable of using people in any way he wants. We may not think a waiter should have a powerful miracle-ministry, but God might. We must not restrict him.

Opposition soon turns up, apparently from those who shared Stephen's Greek language and cultural background. These Jews call themselves free but are bound by prejudice and fear of this new teaching. They try to argue with this Christian worker but he has been well taught by the apostles and speaks with the power of the Spirit. They cannot defeat his argument, but where logic and truth fail them, deceit and treachery come to their rescue. They recruit some false witnesses, lobby the religious leadership and kidnap Stephen to bring him to the Council (not a body of men noted for their warmth towards the Christians – see 5:18, 33). Things continue to go downhill for Stephen as the false witnesses repeat and enlarge on their allegations in front of the Sanhedrin. Their charges are not so much complete fabrications as grotesque distortions of what he had said. (They had made precisely the same charge about Jesus (Matthew 26:61), twisting his words also.) Despite all this pressure Stephen remains calm and assured – God's Spirit giving him the appearance of an angel. There is more than a touch of irony here: Moses is under threat, Stephen's accusers say and yet the description of Stephen parallels that of Moses having just had his meeting with God (Exodus 34:29).

Notice how the freed men are totally unconcerned about whether the message of Stephen is true or not. It threatens their position and perhaps even their safety (what if people assume they are linked with Stephen because of their shared culture and language?). Stephen must be stopped. Truth must not be allowed to get in the way of comfort and security!

Questions

1. How do we behave when our comfort and security are threatened? How can we be open to new ideas, correction or anything else which makes us feel undervalued?
2. Should our churches be growing numerically (verses 1, 7)? If so, how should this be happening? How can we play our part?
3. How far should the church have the same structures as secular organizations? How should they differ?

Acts 7:1–19

Stephen's defence: the faith of our ancestors

The longest speech in the book of Acts begins. Stephen describes some highlights from Jewish history – starting with Abraham – all leading to Jesus.

Abraham (verses 1–9)

After hearing from the accusers (6:13–14) the high priest turns his attention to the defence. Stephen is invited to confess his guilt or deny it; he chooses to

launch into a major speech, drawing on significant portions of
the Old Testament to establish his case. It's important to
understand that this is not an academic lecture on Jewish history.
Some important incidents are missed out and some of the
information seems a bit muddled when we look back to the Old
Testament itself. This is a man arguing for his life in the cauldron
of treachery which the Council meeting had become. We are a
million miles from the detached objectivity of the lecture room!
The thrust of the argument is what is vital, not the neat
arrangement of the material.

After a respectful, almost warm, greeting, 'brothers and
fathers', Stephen begins his defence with Abraham, one of the
earliest and most significant people in all of Jewish history.
Stephen describes how *faith* played a significant part in
Abraham's life. Without knowing where he was going he was
to set off (Genesis 12:1)! Given all the dangers of travel in the
ancient world this journey would have been reckless, even
foolish, had it not been a step of faith in response to a word from
God. There are important lessons here. To act 'in faith' when God
has *not* spoken is reckless and irresponsible. To not act when he
has spoken is disobedient and faithless. Listen and obey.

Abraham also had to exercise faith when he arrived in the land
he was promised. He would not see the fulfilment in his own
life-time, but his descendants, after a period in Egypt (Genesis
15:13–14), would inherit the land. The covenant of circumcision
was then given as a sign of the special relationship between God
and Abraham and his descendants. Romans 4:9f is Paul's
development of Stephen's argument. Abraham exercised faith
which led to circumcision; he did not believe because of
circumcision, circumcision was given because he believed!

All this seems immensely complicated to us. We need to
remember that their history was very, very important to the
Jews. Their ancestors were not just figures of interest, but role-
models to follow. 'If Abraham did it so should we.' Stephen is
trying to demonstrate that if they want to be good Jews they
should remember not only the *result* of Abraham's relationship

with God (they were absorbed by the rite of circumcision and the possession of the land), but also the *cause* of it, *faith* and *obedience* (cf. 3:17; 4:19).

Joseph and Moses (verses 9-19)

Moving on from Abraham Stephen takes the Council into the life of Joseph. His brothers (patriarchs = sons of Jacob) hated him because they were jealous of his favour with his father (Genesis 34:3) and his vivid dreams which showed them bowing down to him (Genesis 34:10-11). God was not deflected from his purpose for Joseph, he simply used a heathen ruler in a foreign country to provide for him. Such was God's care for his people that he told Joseph to prepare for famine seven years before it happened (Genesis 41:25-32) and made sure his father heard about this provision at the right time (Genesis 42:2). Despite this famine, and the later deceit and oppression of the Pharaoh, God continued to provide for his people.

The thrust of Stephen's argument was that God was bigger than the Jews' obsession with their land. Stephen does not deny that they have been promised the land, simply that God is not limited by it or constrained within it. He had provided for his people in Joseph's day in *another* land (Egypt is mentioned eight times in the passage, as if to underline this). By focusing so fully on the promise of the land the contemporaries of Stephen are in danger of reducing God to a localized deity, with little interest in anything beyond some narrow geographical boundaries.

So much of later Christian teaching flows from this argument. Stephen could not have realized the significance of his speech for, for example, the concept of the God of the whole world (17:24-28) and the place of non-Jews in the purpose of God (11:1f). Both these themes are picked up and developed later in Acts. Stephen is describing Jewish history in a way which challenges their traditional understanding. He wants to demonstrate that, in his understanding of Jewish history, the arrival of Jesus the Messiah should not have been a total surprise. God has been hinting at it since Abraham, and getting increasingly obvious in those hints as Jewish history moves on through Joseph to Moses.

The Council must have been irritated at this lesson from Jewish history delivered by someone with a Greek name who had been appointed to 'wait on tables' (6:2)! Worse was to come.

Questions

1. How can we discern the difference between faith and foolishness? How can we help each other?
2. What can we learn from the history of the Old Testament and from the story of the church? Why is it important?
3. 'My country, right or wrong.' What does this passage imply about an attitude like this?

Acts 7:20–50

Jesus, greater than our ancestors

Stephen's speech focuses on Moses, perhaps the most respected figure in Jewish history. The evidence for Jesus the Messiah continues to grow.

God's servant Moses (verses 20–32)

Stephen begins by reminding the Council of the miraculous preservation of Moses in the early months of his life (Exodus 2:1–10). He honours his great stature, 'no ordinary child', and his gifting, 'powerful in speech and action'. Stephen may well have had the comments of his accusers in mind (6:11, 14) when he speaks of Moses in such glowing terms.

What follows in the next verses picks up the theme begun in the last section. God is bigger than their concern about the land – their beloved Palestine. Moses was born outside it, educated outside it, had a home outside it, was commissioned outside it and exercised his ministry outside it. Egypt, Midian, Mount Sinai and Egypt again, were all places where God was obviously present and chose to act decisively and powerfully. Of course, all these facts would be known to the Council, but the *implications* of these facts had either been missed or ignored. Stephen's case here hangs on his interpretation of history. One particular aspect of God's plan, his promise of the land, has been emphasized to the detriment of many other parts of his purpose, for example, the coming of the Messiah. Stephen's contemporaries have read the Old Testament through the tinted lenses of the 'land pre-occupation' – he invites them to take off their glasses and give the material a fresh look!

One of the small phrases in this passage which we should not miss occurs when Stephen speaks of the 'wisdom of the Egyptians' (verse 22) so positively. The Jews were an insular race who would have found the thought of wisdom in other cultures difficult to take, especially when it was a culture they loved to hate. Emphasizing that their beloved Moses was dependent on a foreign culture for his education (and a foreign woman for his upbringing) must have stuck in their throats. Religious purity was one thing, but first-century Judaism often descended into a narrow nationalism. Stephen is obviously committed to the separation which protects from compromise, but not to a separation which produced bigotry and arrogance.

Notice also the short phrase in verse 30 – 'after forty years'. Moses waited a long time before God's purpose was revealed. We do well to remind ourselves that God's timetable may be different from ours (2 Peter 3:8–9)!

God's servant Moses rejected (verses 33–50)

Stephen's speech continues with the theme of rejection – already hinted at (Joseph – verse 9; Moses – verse 25) – it is going to be one of the major points in Stephen's summing up. This rejection of Moses was not confined to the start of his ministry. Even after incredible miracles, the plagues and the crossing of the Red Sea, they still reject him as leader. In the process they reject his deliverance from Egypt and they reject his God. This whole sorry stage in Israelite history (which sowed the seeds for future idolatry and rebellion (cf. Amos 5:25–27) occurred because God's chosen rescuer, Moses, was rejected.

'Make no mistake about it,' Stephen says, 'Moses was great, really great but he pointed forward to someone else.' This person would be one of them, a Jew, with a rescue-ministry, just like Moses. (You can almost feel the Sanhedrin getting increasingly concerned and irritated as the implications of some of these statements begin to dawn on them!)

Moses had just received the law – 'living words' Stephen calls them – when the rejection of Moses and the idolatry began. Stephen's two words to describe the law indicate his belief in their divine origin and in their relevance to human life. His accusers were wide off the mark (6:13); his view of the law was not destructive or negative.

In the years which followed the life of Moses God's presence was identified with a large tent (the tabernacle). This went with the people of Israel in the wilderness, over the Jordan and into the promised land. It lasted through the entire period of the Judges, through Saul's kingship and David's until he proposed a temple to replace it. The project was completed by David's son, Solomon. God, however, was bigger than the splendid temple built for him (Isaiah 66:1): it could not contain him. He had created everything (Isaiah 66:2) – not even heaven and earth were big enough!

The Jews placed great emphasis on the law and the temple. Stephen points out the limitations of both. The law (even with

Moses present) did not stop a full-scale rebellion against God. The temple, magnificent though it was, could not begin to contain the Almighty. None of the traditional emphases were enough to express all of God.

Questions

1. Can a Christian worship an idol? What do 'idols' look like in our day?
2. Is our God too small? In what ways do we try to limit or contain him?
3. In what ways do we reject God's messengers today? What are the results (see verses 39–40)?

Acts 7:51 – 8:8

Martyrdom, persecution and power

Stephen dies as a martyr and his death releases a tidal wave of persecution. But martyrdom is not the only kind of witness, as Philip demonstrates.

Stephen's witness to God's glory (verses 51 – 8:1a)

And so Stephen concludes his speech. He has
painstakingly built up his evidence to arrive at the conclusion that the excessive preoccupation of his contemporaries with the land, the law and the temple, worthy though they are, has blinded them to the significance of Jesus the Messiah. Despite

claiming to be students of the Old Testament they have missed, ignored or misunderstood this vital strand in its teaching.

In these verses Stephen moves from defence to attack. Using language reminiscent of the ancient prophets (cf. Exodus 33:5; Isaiah 63:10), he accuses them of being just like the rebellious Israelites of old. Like their ancestors they resist God, reject his messengers and have now gone so far as to reject the Messiah – by killing him. This last accusation must have stung. The Council has heard it *twice* before from Peter (4:10; 5:30). What is more, even by their own standards (the law) they have disobeyed God.

They are wild with anger (Christians seemed to have this effect on the Sanhedrin; cf. 5:33), contorting their faces and mouths in rage. Stephen, by contrast, is serene and peaceful; a vision of his Messiah with God the Father fills his mind. The words of Jesus in Mark 14:62 may well have prompted this experience. The Council can stand it no longer. They cover their ears, scream abuse at Stephen and drag him off to be bludgeoned to death by rocks and stones at the edge of the city.

Stephen dies as he has lived, filled with the Holy Spirit, with a prayer on his lips for his killers and a commitment of himself back to God. In many ways he reminds us of Jesus: his lack of resistance, his serene spirit and his dying words (cf. Luke 23:34, 46). He is the first Christian martyr, he will not be the last. His courage and bearing have strengthened many down the centuries in their final hours.

Twice in this section Luke mentions someone who will come to dominate the last part of Acts and tower over the development of the early church, a young man named Saul. He guards the cloaks of the executioners and approves of the death of this Christian 'heretic'. But God will have the final word in his life!

Christians are under physical attack (verses 8:1b–3)

The stoning of Stephen seems to have unleashed all the pent-up frustration and anger which was felt by many Orthodox Jews.

Jerusalem had ceased to be a safe place for followers of Jesus, so they found themselves fleeing into the countryside and towns around the city, Judea, or pushing further north to settle in Samaria. The apostles (probably 'the twelve') remained in the city to continue to provide a headquarters for the developing Christian movement. It is not clear how they avoided arrest. Perhaps they were in semi-hiding, protected by the goodwill of ordinary people (cf. 5:13).

Stephen is not forgotten. 'Godly men' gave him a decent burial and there was obviously much sadness. Luke seems to imply that these men were not part of the early church. They could have been Pharisees, like Gamaliel, who felt that the Council's reaction had been rash and ill-advised. It is possible that remorse may have set in among more 'open', sensitive members of the Sanhedrin. Certainly no such remorse appeared to be worrying Saul, who threw himself into persecuting the church with systematic, hateful enthusiasm. This was a door-to-door campaign of a different sort! No-one was safe from his violence: homes and privacy were violated, even the women received no mercy.

Persecution spreads the Good News! (verses 4–8)

While all this was going on, one of Stephen's colleagues on the diaconate had found his way to Samaria. Like other Christian refugees Philip gave himself whole-heartedly to the evangelistic task. Just like Stephen (6:8) he found he had a far wider and more powerful ministry than food distribution. The apostles' commissioning (6:6) had released power and new ministries in him (cf. 2 Timothy 1:6). The expressions of healing power made people pay 'close attention' to his message. Various individuals were released from crippling physical conditions and the grip of Satan was broken in many lives. No wonder they were delighted to have Philip!

The amazing irony is that the persecution is having the opposite effect from the one intended. Far from being contained the gospel message is spreading just as Jesus said it would (1:8; cf. 8:1). And to the Samaritans of all people, sworn enemies of the Jews; they hated each other (cf. John 4:9). The Good News is already crossing cultural, religious and racial boundaries, bringing healing and forgiveness.

Questions

1. Do you think Stephen's example played a part in Saul's conversion? List the people who played a part in yours and thank God for them.
2. How can we learn to forgive our enemies when we feel more like revenge?
3. Which countries/groups are trying to 'destroy the church' (verse 3)? Share information about how successful they are. (You will need some prepared material here; items from magazines, newspapers, missionary letters etc.).

Acts 8:9–25

Magic and money encounter the Truth

Philip continues his ministry and comes into contact with a local sorcerer. The apostles arrive, Peter and John introduce the power of the Holy Spirit and the sorcerer is silenced.

Simon the magician: is he converted? (verses 9–14)

Luke now introduces us to a new character: Simon. Philip may have seen Simon as a rival for the attention of the Samaritans. Both of them do astounding things which amaze the people . . . but there the similarity ends.

➤ Simon's displays of wonder are called 'magic', Philip's are called 'miracles'.

➤ Simon talks about himself, Philip talks about God.

➤ After Simon's 'magic' people follow *him*, after Philip's 'miracles' people follow Jesus!

That Simon could do amazing tricks was not in question. Even assuming that the people of Samaria were a little gullible, we are still dealing with an impressive personality displaying remarkable powers. The Samaritans certainly thought he was some kind of god or, at least, the special representative of a god. He cannot have been thrilled when the people switched allegiance to Philip and his message about the kingdom of God. Simon is very impressed by Philip's power and hovers at his side constantly, presumably to work out how the 'magic' works.

Simon has seen the people's response to Philip and assumes that this is the first step to getting Philip's power; he himself is baptized.

It is very difficult indeed to know if Simon's 'conversion' is genuine. Surely Philip would have spotted a 'con' or act of pretence? On the other hand, his motives don't seem to be pure – like those in Jesus' day who 'believed' on the basis of the miracles they had seen (John 2:23–25). Jesus did not trust them! Neither does the description which Peter gives him easily fit someone who is a genuine believer. Perhaps he is so obsessed with his search for power that he is partially blinded to his own motives; he believes in Jesus to obtain another source of power. God will not be used in this way.

When the apostles in Jerusalem hear about how the gospel is making inroads into the Samaritan community, they send Peter and John to check it out. It would have been thrilling for them to see the words of Jesus coming true (1:8) and the gospel being released among their (previously hated) northern neighbours. Peter and John are keen to witness this remarkable development with their own eyes. The Samaritan believers would need to be assured of their acceptance, and given an apostolic stamp of approval!

Simon the manipulator: is he convinced? (verses 15–25)

The 'normal' pattern of believing in Jesus and receiving the Spirit seems to have been altered on this occasion. It's doubtful that Philip's ministry is defective and they have to wheel in the big guns to put it right. More likely, the Spirit is withheld until a closer bonding between Jerusalem believers and Samaritan believers can be expressed in the presence of Peter and John. At this stage in the expansion of Christianity it would be devastating for the Samaritans to encounter the Spirit without 'encountering' their fellow Jewish believers. Baptism is into one body (1 Corinthians 12:13), not two – Jewish Christians *and* Samaritan

Christians. 'Normally', believing and receiving would happen together; this unique missionary situation needed an alternative pattern.

When Simon sees the power of Peter and John (he seems to have been a spectator not a participant) he attempts to buy their apostolic status so that he too can release the power of the Spirit into people's lives. There seems to have been some visible sign as the apostles prayed (tongues? vibrant joy? great emotion?) and no doubt Simon also believed it to be the key which unlocked the kind of power he had seen Philip exercise.

Peter rounds on Simon immediately with a blunt condemnation of both his action and his attitude. Actually he seems to get away with it quite lightly compared with Ananias and Sapphira (5:1–11)! The apostles cannot be 'bought' and neither can God's power. Repentance is Simon's only hope. Far from being someone great he was a slave, in bondage to his own motives and desires. Full of smouldering resentments Simon is stunned by this verbal assault, but not motivated to repentance. His request to Peter is only an attempt to avoid further punishment: he shows no sign of a genuine change of heart.

This story acts as a potent reminder of the dangers of counterfeit faith. So much about Simon seems to indicate a change of heart. How many of us have known those who make some kind of 'decision' for Christ, they may even have made it to baptism or confirmation, but who soon reveal their faith as defective? Their 'decision' was to please a parent, get a child baptized or continue a relationship – Jesus was never the end, only the means!

Peter and John returned south to Jerusalem taking the opportunity to evangelize as they went. What exciting news they had to share with their fellow apostles – the gospel was spreading and the church was growing.

Questions

1. Jealousy played a big part in Simon's downfall. Why is it so dangerous? How do we spot it in ourselves? What can we do to conquer it?
2. Should we expect the miraculous in our evangelism? What problems might it cause?
3. Why do we follow Jesus/worship God? Each make a list and share the results. Notice how many reasons given are 'us-centred' ('he makes us happy, peaceful, saves us . . .') and how many 'God-centred' ('he is the truth, holy, almighty . . .') What can we learn from the exercise?

Acts 8:26–40

Philip and the Ethiopian

Philip is supernaturally commissioned to meet an Ethiopian, to witness to him. Conversion and baptism follow his presentation of the Good News.

 Fresh from the excitement of the crowds in Samaria Philip is now given a divine assignment to an individual. It is about 50 miles from Jerusalem to Gaza and the road runs through desert as it heads south, reaching the city of Gaza itself. As he travels Philip meets up with an African from the South Sahara (Sudan?) who is chancellor of the exchequer for Candace (a title, not a name), ruler of Ethiopia. He is a 'eunuch' (though probably this is an official title, not a physical description denoting the removal of his sexual organs), and must have been a convert to Judaism because he has been up to Jerusalem to worship and he has obtained a copy of Isaiah – both would be extremely difficult for a Gentile to do. Besides, Luke views Cornelius as the first gentile convert (11:1).

Prompted by the Holy Spirit Philip approaches this high-ranking official and starts chattering about the book the Ethiopian seems to be about two-thirds of the way through. 'Do you understand Isaiah 53:78?,' Philip asks. 'No, but climb in and tell me about it,' he replies. This important man is gracious and humble, obviously ready to learn, so Philip uses Isaiah to point the way to Jesus. Stephen has already used the Old Testament to the same effect with a crowd (the Council); now Philip uses the same technique with an individual. Jesus is the key to understanding the Old Testament Scriptures; they, in turn, point forward to his coming.

The message of Philip is obviously heard and understood, and baptism is requested when he sees an oasis by the side of the road. After the baptism Philip disappears, adding a supernatural ending to a story with a supernatural start and continues his preaching ministry to the north in Azotus. From there he travels north, evangelizing coastal towns on the 60-mile journey to Caesarea. The Ethiopian cannot see Philip but he can 'see' Jesus! He returns to Africa 'rejoicing' in his newly-found faith.

The gospel makes another advance: first the Jews, then the Samaritans, now a black African in a position of great influence. Jesus certainly died but he is not dead – his power and message continue to change lives.

Questions

1. Baptism is obviously important in Acts (verse 36; cf. 2:38, 41). Have you been baptized? Why is it important?
2. Notice the three divine 'nudges' Philip got in this story (verses

26, 29, 39). Why is it important to be sensitive to the Holy Spirit in evangelism? How can we learn to listen to him as we witness?

3. Isaiah was talking about Jesus and so was Philip. Who are we talking about? Does Jesus feature strongly in our conversations and lives? Why?/Why not?

A gospel for everyone

Jesus leaves his disciples with a promise and a command about the spread of the Good News (Acts 1:8). It is a remarkable statement to make to Jews who, in the main, saw God's blessing reserved only for them. As the story of the church unfolds in Acts we see the gospel reaching out to more and more people. These people are not only distant from Jerusalem geographically, but also in culture, religion, race and colour.

Luke shows us the message of Jesus breaking down barriers of every kind:

- the hated Samaritans respond to the Good News (8:4f; cf. John 4:9);

- a black African Eunuch is converted (8:26f), as is an 'unclean' Gentile (10:44–48);

- women discover Christ (9:36) and are used by him in ministry (21:9).

Almost all the prejudices of a first-century Jew are confronted. No-one is barred, everyone is welcome, the gospel knows no 'exclusion zones'.

Acts 9:1–19a

Saul's U-turn

A persistent persecutor of God's people is stopped in his tracks. Jesus confronts Saul on the road to Damascus – a dramatic conversion results and Saul is a changed man.

God intervenes (verses 1–9)

Saul may well have been more moved by the death of Stephen than he cares to admit (7:58; 8:1). But if he was he certainly is not admitting it to anyone – especially not to himself! He redoubles his already fanatical harassment of the Christians by asking permission to go into Eastern Syria, to one of the major towns, in order to continue his mission. The Jewish Council had no authority politically in Syria, but would have had significant influence over the *Jews* living in Damascus (there may have been over 20,000 at this stage of the first century). Saul is determined to bring to 'justice' all these followers of 'the Way' (cf. John 14:6) – they need not think that by running over 150 miles away they would escape detection!

As Saul got near to the end of his journey to Damascus, he was put in God's spotlight in no uncertain terms. Light more sudden and bright than lightning 'knocked' him to the ground and a voice enquired about why Saul was persecuting him. Saul is no doubt very confused (this seems to be God's voice, but Saul is not persecuting God; he is defending his honour, isn't he?) and not a little afraid. In a state of confusion and fear he stutters out a request to know the identity of the voice. He must have been totally stunned by the reply, devastated emotionally by the implications of the words. All this time he has been opposing the work of God and doing the opposite of what he thought he was doing. For a man of Saul's intensity this must have been an incredible shock to the system.

The voice (Jesus) then tells Saul to go into Damascus and wait for further instructions. All this time his assistants were stunned into silence; they heard vague sounds, but could not eavesdrop on the conversation between Saul and Jesus, or see anyone but Saul. Saul staggers to his feet only to discover that the light has blinded him. This gives him no choice but to obey the voice, spending three days recovering from the shock and trying to work out what it all means. Saul, the strong, confident persecutor has met his match.

Ananias into the lion's den (verses 10–19a)

Ananias seems to have lived in Damascus for some time although how he became a Christian we are not told. He was obviously a committed follower of Jesus whom God spoke to in a vision with instructions about Saul. Saul was a broken man – spiritually turned around, emotionally stunned and physically disabled – but Ananias has only a hint of all this. He can hardly believe that God is sending him into the lion's den . . . to help the lion! 'Don't you know, Lord, that this is the man who has damaged your church in Jerusalem and has come here to do the same?'

The Lord did know this and still wants Ananias to go! Saul was to be a key agent for God's kingdom. He would preach before Jews and Gentiles, even having opportunities to address their rulers. But this high calling would have its cost: Saul would not have a life of ease and comfort. So Ananias went. It is important to understand the courage and level of obedience of the Damascan disciple. Would he be ambushed by Saul's assistants? Once in the house of Judas how would he get out? How would his fellow Christians feel about him helping their sworn enemy? Despite all these questions (and the anxiety that went with them) Ananias still does what Jesus tells him.

Saul is praying and Ananias immediately affirms him as a brother in Christ. He has come on the instruction of Jesus to bring physical healing and spiritual release. Luke does not tell us about what, if any, signs followed Saul's filling with the Spirit (cf. 2:4; 4:31), but it is certain the prayer of Ananias was effective. Saul's physical sight is restored and his new spiritual sight is expressed in baptism. Once he starts to eat again he returns to full physical health and strength. ('Straight street' (verse 11) was a prestigious road with substantial housing – perhaps there was a pool in the courtyard.)

The order of events – Holy Spirit-filling followed by baptism – is the reverse of the Samaritan experience (8:12, 17). It is hard to escape the conclusion that in these early days of church life, the *order* of events in becoming a Christian is nowhere near as important as the *reality* of each component part.

Questions

1. 'It doesn't matter what you believe as long as you are sincere.' What does this passage have to say about this statement? What would you say if someone said it to you?
2. Should we all have a 'Damascus Road' experience? Does conversion need to be dramatic?
3. Why is there so much emphasis in Acts on being filled with the Holy Spirit (verse 17)? Is there too much or too little emphasis on this today?
4. For Saul, success and suffering would go hand in hand (verses 15–16). Is this a 'rule' of the Christian life? How far is our lack of success because of our fear of suffering?

God's Spirit in charge

**God works wonders, literally, in making
Saul a new man and bringing life back
to a dead woman, through Peter.**

An enthusiastic convert
(verses 9b–31)

This is a really remarkable about-face. After a
few days consulting with the Christian community in Damascus
Saul launches into a vigorous and enthusiastic proclamation of
the gospel. In what appears to be little more than a week he has
gone from being a Christ-denying, bigoted Pharisee to announ-
cing to the Jewish community that Jesus really is the Christ. An
amazing 'U-turn'! Only the power of God can explain this.

So incredible is this conversion that both the Jews and the
Christians have trouble believing it! Now nobody trusts him
easily. But Saul is unstoppable; his religious education and
training coupled with his dramatic experience make him a
formidable debater against the orthodox Jewish opposition. He
could show beyond reasonable doubt ('proving') that Jesus was
who he said he was. The sound of the Pharisee-turned-traitor
becomes too much for the Jews to bear, so they plan to have him
killed. Their plot is foiled by the clever use of a basket and some
rope; not a very dignified method of transport for a religious
leader but Saul is going to have to get used to far worse things in
the future!

Luke is only giving us a summary of Saul's life at this point –
not every detail. He tells us nothing about going to Arabia
(Galatians 1:17) and then back to Damascus. When Luke writes

his account he is not concerned with filling in all the biographical details of Saul's life – these are simply the 'recorded highlights'. It is three years before Saul arrives in Jerusalem (Galatians 1:18) and even then he is treated with suspicion. Fortunately Barnabas the encourager is on hand to act as go-between. Barnabas tells them about Saul's experience of Jesus and Saul is accepted by the Jerusalem church. He continues to preach and debate about Jesus, but his life is threatened again. The believers decide that for his own safety he ought to be out of Jerusalem and they send him home to Tarsus.

This is followed by a period of relative calm in the relationship between the Christians and the Jews. The church uses this time to recover from persecution, God graciously continues to give encouraging signs of his presence and numerical growth results.

Peter's power ministry (verses 32–43)

Luke picks up the story of Peter where he left him (8:25) – preaching the gospel. He goes to a town 25 miles north-west of Jerusalem to encourage the Christians. He discovers a man who is so badly paralysed that he has been bed-bound for eight years. Peter heals him in the name of Jesus (cf. 3:6) and tells him to put his sleeping mat away; from now on he will only need it at night. Aeneas was a remarkable testimony to God's healing power, and lots of people in Lydda and northward into neighbouring Sharon came to Christ as a result.

At the port of Joppa, 35 miles away, a very special lady was dying. This woman was always making clothing for the poor and caring for them in a range of different ways. With no state provision widows were often some of the poorest members of the community (cf. James 1:27). No wonder they were so distraught when she died; Dorcas would be badly missed. The believers in Joppa respond to this emergency by sending two of their number inland to ask Peter to come from Lydda. Peter may well have remembered how Jesus dealt with the daughter of

Jairus because he handles the situation in a very similar way . . . and the result is the same (Mark 5:38–42).

Peter then presents the very alive Dorcas to two significant groups: the *Christians* to encourage their faith and the *widows* to assure them of further help in the fight against poverty. Both groups – perhaps for different reasons – would have been thrilled. The result of this 'resurrection' was a significant rise in the number of Christians in the region. The raising of Lazarus had similar results (cf. John 12:10–11). Peter then stayed on in Joppa, presumably to assist with the discipleship of the new converts and to continue preaching the gospel. He was even happy to stay with Simon whose contact with dead animals made him 'unclean' as far as the Jewish rabbis were concerned. In addition the tanner's job was often associated with dirt and a pungent smell and the general population may have avoided him for this reason.

So Peter stays with Simon: a man rejected by the Jews and snubbed by the rest of the community finds acceptance in the Christian church.

Questions

1. Do you think that Peter was able to raise Dorcas because he used the same method as Jesus? Similar words? Or was it something else?
2. Barnabas brought the two sides together (verse 27). Why is the message of reconciliation so important? How can we apply it in our own circumstances?
3. Sometimes it is right to stay and fight (e.g., 5:40–41). Sometimes to leave the trouble-spot (verse 30). How can we know when to do which?

Acts 10:1–23a

Peter sent to a Gentile

**God speaks to a Roman centurion by an
angel, and to Peter by a vision, with
a view to getting them together.**

Cornelius and the angel (verses 1–8)

This next section in Acts describes a major
advance in the spread of the gospel: Jews
with a Hebrew or Greek background (6:1), the 'half-Jews' of
Samaria (8:1), an African-Jewish convert (8:27) . . . and now a
Gentile. It is nothing short of miracle that a faith which grew out
of Judaism could be offered to Gentiles so quickly!

Cornelius lived in the port of Caesarea, the Roman capital of
Judea, which was about 65 miles north-west of Jerusalem. It
needed a Roman cohort of about 600 men to protect the harbour
area, the city's administrative buildings and the vital water
supply brought by aqueduct into the city. Cornelius was neither
a Jew nor a Jewish convert, but he was a kind, generous and
deeply religious man and so were his family. During mid-
afternoon prayer, in broad daylight, he saw an angel who calls
him by name. It is all he can do to stutter out a simple question in
his panic (a very similar response to Saul – 9:5). God had noted
his kindness to the poor and his spiritual devotion. He is told to
send for Peter who is 30 miles away in Joppa, living by the sea-
shore. They would have had to ask for Simon's house when they
arrived in Joppa – or perhaps they just followed their noses (see
above).

Many of Cornelius' servants obviously share his spiritual
leanings, as do some of his soldiers, and after sharing his

'angelic' experience with them he sends three off on the errand. The soldiers' presence is primarily for physical protection but also adds a certain 'official' authority as they travel; and particularly as they tried to obtain accommodation on the way and directions to Simon's house, once in Joppa.

It is interesting to note in Luke's account of the growth of the church that Dorcas and Cornelius have two things in common. Firstly, both are from groups of people you would never expect to be commended in a Jewish culture – women and Gentiles. It is almost as if the gospel delights in working with the under-dog (see p. 54). Secondly, both are commended for their work among the poor, an activity which always has the blessing of Jesus because it was part of his ministry (Luke 4:18).

Peter's revolutionary vision (verses 9–23a)

The messengers make good time from Caesarea and by noon the next day are approaching the outskirts of Joppa. At this time, Peter is making his way on to the roof of the house (looking for shade and the cool of the sea-breeze?) to pray. He is extremely hungry and while lunch is being made for him he falls into some kind of trance. Luke calls what he experiences a 'vision' (as had Cornelius) though it is difficult to know if he is dreaming, day-dreaming or put in some kind of 'unearthly state' by God. Whichever it is, Peter 'sees' a sheet with animals in it, some of them banned by Jewish law (Leviticus 11: 1–47) which he is told to eat. God tells him that God has made these animals clean so he can eat them. This is repeated three times.

Peter is confused by this vision, but God has the messengers from Cornelius outside to help unravel the mystery. Peter is to leave the roof and respond positively to their request to go to Cornelius. He identifies himself and asks what these travellers want. The men describe their master and explain about the vision Cornelius has had. They hope Peter will be persuaded by Cornelius' character and by his good standing among Jews to come with them. If not, they hope he will be convinced by the story of an angel visiting their master despite the fact that he is a Gentile. As it happens, Peter has already been instructed to do this by an even higher authority than Cornelius! Peter (presumably with Simon's permission!) invites the travellers into the house for food, refreshment and a good night's sleep after their journey up the coast.

For Peter the meaning of the vision is slowly becoming clear. It was not really about what food he could eat or who he could eat it with; it was a vision of far deeper significance. How deep he could not have realized at this point. All his preconceptions about God's plan and purpose with regard to the Gentiles was about to change radically. And this shift in his thinking came neither by his human wisdom and initiative, nor by some strategic mission plan thought up by the apostles. This is God's work and Luke is at pains to highlight the supernatural aspects of change of heart which opened up the Gentile mission field.

Questions

1. Prayer plays an important part in the life of Cornelius. What state is your prayer life in? How can it be developed?
2. Does God still speak through angel visits and 'trances'? Why are these forms of guidance so rare?
3. Do you think Christians have traditions and customs that have grown up over the years? What are they? Do they put people off the church?

Acts 10:23b–48

Gentiles are God's people too!

Peter travels to Caesarea, meets Cornelius and preaches Christ to the Gentiles. There is an amazing response and a new era in the life of the church begins.

Peter and Cornelius meet at last (verses 23b–33)

After a good night's rest (though for Peter it may have been filled with unanswered questions, and no doubt, some more prayer!) the group of ten (see 11:12) set off for Caesarea. The 30-mile journey takes a little longer going back and the group do not arrive until the next day.

Cornelius is ready for them, and has assembled quite a crowd of his family members and friends. He obviously senses that this is an occasion of great significance and wants to share it with those close to him. Peter arrives and Cornelius bows in deep reverence to him: this is not simply a mark of respect, but more like 'worship'. Peter is not used to this treatment (he may have thought it close to idolatry) and encourages Cornelius to stand up (cf. Revelation 19:9–10). The instruction to summon Peter to come may have been supernatural, but Peter is only too aware of his humanness – 'I am only a man'; reverence of this kind belongs only to God.

Going inside Peter finds a large and expectant congregation. 'I shouldn't really be here,' he admits, 'but I've had a vision which told me God's assessment of people was more important than mine. I have come in obedience to him, without raising any of the usual objections a Jew would raise in these circumstances. How can I help you?' This really was a remarkable speech from a first-century Jew. It shows how much the vision was altering his viewpoint and how he is beginning to grasp its significance.

Cornelius then explains how the invitation to Peter came about. Peter has heard most of this from the messengers, but the repetition no doubt helps fill in some of the details and also ensures that everyone in the large gathering knows the background to the meeting. Cornelius thanks Peter for coming and expresses the belief that God is present in the room, that he wants to speak through Peter and that the assembled crowd is ready to listen.

This speech is almost as remarkable as Peter's! A Roman military leader speaking to a Jew (in front of witnesses) in such a humble way, is amazing. He shows outstanding spiritual insight and openness.

The Gentiles believe! (verses 34–48)

Peter opens his sermon with a confession, admitting how he has come to realize his mistaken thinking about the Gentiles. 'God has no favourites' is a total climb-down for a Jew, who had probably been brought up to believe that he was part of God's favourite nation. The Jews were a 'chosen' people, of course, but this was not meant to imply a special *status*, simply a special *opportunity*, that through them the nations of the world could be blessed. God could accept people irrespective of their place of birth or nationality.

The 'meat' of Peter's sermon contains many of the same elements he has used before (2:14f; 3:11f). These repeated themes (for example, 'Jesus is God's chosen Messiah', 'we are the witness', etc.) form the foundation of apostolic preaching over these early years. They are a presentation of historical facts with an invitation to respond to their implications. That is, if Jesus really did do all these things and he really is alive (and the apostles have seen this with their own eyes: see 1 John 1:1–2); if he is the unique chosen one, the only 'logical' response is to believe and follow him.

This sermon of Peter's laid more stress than some of his others on the life and ministry of Jesus. Perhaps a Gentile congregation in Caesarea needed more reminding about this than the Jews in Jerusalem. The ministry of Jesus occurred in a very small geographical area (his trip to Egypt as a baby may have been the farthest he ever went; Matthew 2:13) and it would have been a mistake to assume that some in this Gentile audience knew any more about Jesus than the haziest of details.

Peter's sermon ends with the beginnings of an appeal (cf. 2:38), but he appears to be interrupted by the Holy Spirit. 'While Peter was *still* speaking.' The six Jewish Christians can hardly believe their eyes and ears; the theory of Peter's sermon ('God has no favourites') is dramatically put into practice and the Holy Spirit is poured out on these Gentiles, just as on them. There is no reason to prohibit baptism into both Christ and the Christian community. Peter stays on for a few days to express commitment to them and no doubt continues the discipleship process.

Questions

1. Cornelius gets family and friends together to hear the gospel (verse 24) and he isn't even a Christian! How can we communicate the gospel better to our friends and families? (Using our homes?)

2. Humility is a key feature in both what Peter says (verses 28–29) and in what Cornelius says (verses 30–32).Why is humility important? How can it be encouraged and developed?

3. 'Tongues' are a common (though not universal) sign of the work of the Spirit in Acts. Why is this? What emphasis should we give this gift today?

Acts 11:1–18

Peter in hot water

The Jewish Christians criticize Peter for being too free with the gospel. He explains how God's Spirit led him, the leaders accept his explanation and praise God.

A storm of protest (verses 1–10)

News of the amazing events in Caesarea seem to have reached Jerusalem before Peter did. Unlike the modern world information travelled slowly. It was communicated as quickly as a man could walk (or ride) to the required destination. It could have taken well over a week for anyone in the capital to hear of these events on the coast, and even then the details may have been 'sketchy'. Peter may have taken several weeks to stay in Caesarea, preach at various towns on the way, and eventually arrive in Jerusalem.

They were waiting impatiently! When he arrived, to a storm of protest from his colleagues, he was immediately called on to explain his actions. The leadership of the church were clearly rattled by what they had heard. Christians were enjoying a lull in hostilities with the Jewish authorities (9:32), but this kind of activity was bound to provoke outrage and further persecution. Worse still, Peter was seen as leader of the group so they would all be tainted by his behaviour.

This incident shows how strongly the Jewish culture and perspective still had a grip on hearts and minds in this period of the church's development. Stephen had pointed away from the traditional elements of Judaism: the law, the land, the temple (7:2–53), to the arrival of the Messiah. Philip had taken the gospel to half-Jews, the Samaritans (8:1), and the break with the past continues. Peter is about to push the whole church into a radical step away from its past and into its future!

Peter's defence consists of telling his fellow-leaders *exactly* what happened. News would have arrived from various sources and in the weeks before he came back to Jerusalem rumours would have been rife. Peter wants the issue discussed on the basis of the *facts*. So he recounts precisely what happened to him in Joppa at Simon's house (cf. 10:9–16).

We have now read this account twice. Luke records the details in full for us on both occasions (rather than just giving us a summary of the previous account in this passage). It is such a crucial issue, he even repeats the main point – 'Do not call unclean what God has called clean' – three times (10:15, 28; 11:9).

The Christians are convinced by the facts (verses 11–18)

Verse 11 sees Peter warming to his theme as he recounts the amazing events at Caesarea (cf. 10:17–47). By repeating this information in detail Luke continues to stress the importance of the issue. It is not Peter who is on trial, but the whole future of Christianity. A rejection of what Peter has done will condemn the Christian message, as a variation of Judaism, to the backwaters of history. An acceptance will do nothing less than open Christianity up to the world!

Peter has brought the six members of the church in Joppa, who went with him to Caesarea, back to Jerusalem. He must have known that his actions would cause uproar, so he brings them to give supporting eye-witness evidence . . . not to mention moral support!

You can almost hear the excitement in Peter's voice as the story is retold; even he can hardly believe it really happened. He reminds them of what Jesus said just before his ascension (verse 16; cf. 1:5) about the Holy Spirit. 'If God accepted these Gentiles,' Peter argues, 'How could I do anything else but accept them too.

I couldn't possibly go against what God was saying.'

Peter's case can be summarized as follows: 'God took the initiative, God arranged the circumstances, God poured out his Spirit . . . what would you have done in my situation.' On hearing this they withdraw their accusations and consider their questions answered. And this is no grudging acceptance of Peter's account. There is genuine delight at this evidence of divine activity – they 'praised God'. Even those 'unclean' Gentiles have found favour with God. The phrase *'even the Gentiles'* sounds patronizing to our ears, even arrogant. But we have to remember the huge gulf which existed between Jews and Gentiles. In the light of this, verse 18 is an earth-shaking admission!

We can see that Luke intends us to understand that the Gentiles receive spiritual life on the same basis as the Jews – repentance. In Acts, repentance is seen as the key which unlocks the door into God's blessing (2:38; 3:19; 5:31; verse 18). We would do well to remember this crucial emphasis. A casual 'accepting Jesus as Saviour' is no substitute for genuine repentance and faith. Spiritual power flows only from the latter!

Questions

1. Why is 'rumour' still so common in church life? Why do we criticize (verse 2) without checking our facts?
2. Peter had changed his mind about the Gentiles (verse 9). Do we admit when we are wrong? Are we open to the possibility that we might be wrong? Why do we find this difficult?
3. Why is repentance (verse 18b) stressed so little in church life today? Why is it important? What difference would it make to, for example, our relationships with other Christians?

Acts 11:19–30

The church expands

Barnabas is sent to investigate the new church in Antioch. He encourages them and calls in Saul to help. The name 'Christians' is given to them.

Barnabas sent to Antioch (verses 19–24)

The ripples from Stephen's death (8:1) continue outwards. Phoenicia was an area along the Mediterranean coast, starting 40 miles north of Caesarea and continuing over 150 miles to the north; Cyprus is only accessible by boat, over 250 miles from Jerusalem; Antioch was about 300 miles north of Jerusalem. These distances begin to illustrate how fast the church is growing and how quickly the message is spreading. The bad news of Stephen's death has turned into good news for the transmitting of the gospel. Because news of the 'Cornelius decision' (11:18) had not reached this far the message was still aimed at Jews. There were exceptions to this and no doubt Greeks were an obvious target group because of the common language. Notice that missionaries had come from Cyrene to preach. Cyrene is on the north African coast about 1,000 miles from Jerusalem! Christianity is no longer a local operation. God obviously blessed this missionary activity because many people became Christians.

News eventually reached the apostles (many weeks later?), who wanted to make sure things were being done decently and in order. They would also want to ensure that good foundations were laid and proper structures established – so Barnabas is sent to Antioch (cf. 8:14). What he finds is a genuine work of God which thrills him. He will be able to take a positive report back to base. His only instruction is about remaining 'true to the Lord'. This seems a slightly odd phrase – no other group of converts has been told this in Acts – until we remember the context – Antioch. This was a thriving mega-city of half a million population, the third largest in the Roman empire. It was a sophisticated city of culture with dozens of racial groupings, nationalities, religions and lifestyles mingling together. It was known as a city of vice, almost any perversion could be 'enjoyed' – at a price. Barnabas is keen to keep the new converts 'true' in the face of so many temptations and pressures.

The passage concludes with a glowing tribute to Barnabas, a similar description to that of Stephen (6:5). The apostles could not have sent a better man – Spirit-filled, full of faith, good . . . and an effective evangelist.

Barnabas calls for Saul (verses 25–30)

Barnabas, sensing the strategic importance of Antioch, decides to stay and continue ministry there. But he is aware of the size of the task and remembers that Saul is in his home town of Tarsus (9:30) about 150 miles away. He sets off to find him and brings him back to Antioch. Out of their friendship, begun many months earlier (9:27), a ministry team develops. For a year they engage in vigorous evangelism and discipleship very effectively.

Soon, enough people have responded to the Good News to arouse the attention of the sophisticated population of Antioch, who gave them a nickname, 'Christians'. Initially this was no doubt intended as a term of ridicule, but it quickly caught on. The believers themselves soon saw how appropriate the name was and it stuck (cf. 1 Peter 4:16).

As the year of ministry went on Barnabas and Saul were joined by a group of prophets from Jerusalem. Agabus predicts famine on a massive scale and Luke, writing some time later, adds his own note to tell us how accurate this prophecy was. The

Jerusalem disciples, as a harassed minority, would fare particularly badly in famine; with this in mind a collection is taken up among their less-harassed and probably wealthier fellow believers. They sent the gift with Barnabas and Saul to the leaders back in Judea – the newest disciples giving generously to support the parent-church in its need.

The story of the church at Antioch signals a shift in power away from Jerusalem. Less of the story in Acts will focus on Judea, more on the world beyond its borders; Paul is featured more than Peter; and the base for operations of missionary activity is Antioch, just as much as Jerusalem. The child is outgrowing the parent and all the problems of dealing with adolescence are going to hit the headquarters of established Christianity very soon.

Not only is all this going on, but even the adoption of the name 'Christian' is rapidly distinguishing the believers from Judaism, and to some extent separating them from it. Ties with the past are being cut, rapid expansion makes control difficult – the church is on a roller-coaster of change.

Questions

1. How can we help new converts remain 'true to the Lord' (verse 23)? Why do so many slip away from God and the church?
2. What an amazing prophecy (verse 28)! Is the gift of prophecy for today? What is it for?
3. What nickname would you give your church? Or the 'Christians' in your house group? How can we live up to our original 'nickname'? What does it mean? How do outsiders react to the word? Do we need to abandon it?

Acts 12:1–19a

Peter's miraculous escape

**Herod throws Peter into prison but God
uses the prayers of the church and rescues
him supernaturally. Naturally, however,
the church finds it hard to believe.**

Peter gets out (verses 1–10)

For some reason Herod decides that now is
the time to persecute the church more
vigorously. He was not a popular character, indeed his whole
family had been hated by the Jews. Because of this he seems to
bend over backwards to please the Jews; his offensive against the
church may be part of his desire to keep in with the Jewish
establishment. Anyway, he arrests James on some trumped-up
charge, and has him beheaded. This so delights the Jews that
Herod decides to pick up the top man and have him thrown in
prison. Unfortunately for Herod the show trial will have to be
delayed because no public hearing was possible during the
period of Passover.

This was the anniversary of the death of Jesus and Peter may
well have thought that he was going to die at the same Jewish
feast as his Master, perhaps by the same method! Herod is
anxious not to lose his prize exhibit, so he assigns sixteen
soldiers to guard him, in groups of four, round the clock. Peter is
not going to escape this time (cf. 5:19).

But the church was praying. Luke consistently emphasizes
prayer in Acts and its mention here is yet another reminder of
the divine dimension. Peter's fate is not at the whim of Herod
the Jew-pleaser or the Jewish authorities. Above the power

politics and clamouring for approval a higher force is at work; actually, a higher person is at work. At just the right time, the night before the trial, God intervenes. Peter is sleeping (which shows he had an amazing sense of peace) and has to be jolted awake by the angel (12:7). Despite the fact that he is chained between two soldiers and there are two more guarding him, Peter gets up, puts his shoes and outer clothes on, and follows the angel. He is half-asleep and half-mesmerized, wondering if this is a dream or a vision. No, it is really happening; those guards they are passing are real enough (are the guards asleep? drunk? in a trance?) as is the iron gate which opens 'automatically'. After a few moments of freedom the angel leaves as suddenly as he had arrived. Despite Herod's precautions Peter is free.

Peter can't get in (verses 11–19a)

Peter pinches himself a few times to make sure all this is really happening and it dawns on him just how amazing his escape has been. Herod has been evaded and the Jewish leaders disappointed, and it is God who has done it. Realizing how dangerous it is for him to be out on the streets at night he hurries to a home where Christians live (a young John Mark lives here, later to go with Paul on a missionary journey and write the second gospel) and discovers a prayer meeting going on.

It is a sizeable home and Peter is forced to knock loudly on a locked outer door until Rhoda goes to the door. He tells her who he is and she races back to the prayer meeting with the amazing news, forgetting to let Peter in. This whole scene is the stuff of farce and comedy, no doubt evoking gales of laughter as it was retold throughout the Christian community. 'Peter is at the door', 'O no he isn't', 'O yes he is' . . . and so on! The intensity of the prayer had made Rhoda hallucinate or his angel was paying them a visit. All this time a very real, very frustrated Peter is trying to get off the street, out of danger and into the security of the house.

Perhaps they were not expecting an answer so quickly or in quite this way; but they are totally flabbergasted. At last they let Peter in and eventually settle down enough to hear his story. Once the story is told he asks that James, the brother of Jesus (emerging more and more as a leader in the Jerusalem church) and the other leaders be informed. He then leaves (presumably getting out more easily than he got in) to go to 'another place'. This was probably to a Christian 'safe house' in the Jerusalem area and then much further away, perhaps back to Simon's house in Joppa, or more likely, completely out of Herod's clutches to Antioch, or even to Rome.

If there was a commotion at Mark's house in the night, there was an even greater one at the prison the next morning! Everyone is confused and bewildered. Herod, having lost his means of gaining the applause of the Jewish leaders, is in no mood for mercy. Peter's guards are condemned to death.

Questions

1. A praying church (verse 5). How can we become a church like this? Why are prayer meetings usually so poorly attended?
2. How do we respond when God answers prayer in ways we do not expect? How do we respond when he does not seem to answer at all?
3. Has God got a sense of humour? What do you think he finds funny? Should we laugh more in church?
4. Herod is angry and cruel. How do we handle our anger? What kind of things are said and done because of anger? How can we learn to control our tempers?

Acts 12:19b – 13:3

Barnabas and Saul commissioned

Herod dies, an arrogant man, while Barnabas and Saul submit to the Spirit's directive to take the Good News to fresh lands.

The death of Herod (verses 19b–24)

Herod had a sizeable administrative and military task so affairs of state would have to take priority over keeping well in with Jewish leaders. Besides, he may have found Jerusalem a little claustrophobic for someone used to the freedoms of Rome. Anyway, he goes away from the capital to the coast at Caesarea. Tyre and Sidon are Mediterranean ports about 60 and 85 miles respectively north of Caesarea in Phoenicia. There would have been fierce competition for trade between Caesarea and the two Phoenician ports, and this could have been the source of the friction with Herod. Whatever the cause, the Phoenicians decided to work together and get Herod to the negotiating table. They desperately needed his goodwill because their food supply came largely from Galilee. A personal and trusted servant (and adviser?) helped set up the meeting.

Once the day arrives Herod treats the occasion more like a coronation than a discussion. Dressed in opulent splendour and seated on a throne, he pompously addresses his subjects (and the visiting Phoenicians?). The response to his speech is grovelling flattery – either from his cringing courtiers or from manipulative Phoenicians (or both!). Herod foolishly accepts their acclaim, only to be immediately reminded by God that he is not a god, but a very mortal human – he is struck dead. There has been a lot of speculation about how Herod died. He seems to have been struck with an abdominal or intestinal complaint. A number of round-worms could block internal tubes, ultimately causing death.

Whatever the physical cause of death Luke clearly understands it to be an act of God. The obvious, stated reason for his death is idolatry – he applied to himself what is meant for God alone. He may also be being punished for his persecution of the church. Later Christians would have drawn comfort from this passage as they faced Roman persecution. Many had to give praise to Caesar as a god or die. Herod 'did not give praise to God' and he died. Their God really is greater than Caesar!

And the gospel goes on flourishing. Roman kings may come and go, political squabbles may dominate things for a while . . . but the 'word of God' outlasts them all (1 Peter 1:24–25).

The first missionaries are called (verses 12:25 – 13:3)

Barnabas and Saul were sent from Antioch with money for the Jewish Christians (11:30). Having done this, they recruit John Mark, the cousin of Barnabas (Colossians 4:10), and return to Antioch.

Luke then lists five key leaders in the Antioch church, describing them as prophets and teachers. Some of the prophets may have been part of the prophetic team from Jerusalem (11:27). These leaders may have had a travelling ministry, but they appear to be based in Antioch, and have some ongoing commitment to the church there. Barnabas and Saul are the familiar names in this list, but the other three are relatively obscure. Their names indicate both the cosmopolitan nature of Antioch and the diversity of background from which converts to Christianity now came. Simeon is a black man, probably from Africa (some people think he may be 'Simon of Cyrene' who carried the cross for Jesus (Luke 23:26)), Lucius was from a north African province and Manaen had political and aristocratic connections.

This diverse quintet provide both the teaching input into the lives of the Christians and the specifically inspirational direction from the Spirit. They may all have had both ministries or, as the original language implies, the first three were prophets and the last two teachers.

Worship and fasting were a regular feature of corporate Christian life and on one of these occasions the Holy Spirit instructed (presumably through a prophetic word from one of the prophets) that Barnabas and Saul be commissioned for a special ministry. No doubt this did not come as a surprise to them, Saul, for example, would have been aware of God's purpose for his life, at least in general terms (cf. 9:15), but it would have been a growing confirmation of their sense of call. The exact nature of the call and place of service is not explained: God will direct them at the right time.

After more praying and fasting, the prophetic word would have to be carefully 'tested' (1 Corinthians 14:29), Barnabas and Saul were commissioned by the laying on of hands (cf. 6:6 – the commissioning of deacons). After this, they were released from their duties in Antioch and sent out on their mission. Here is a divinely chosen team – a prophet and a teacher – to ensure that the word of God continues to spread (12:24).

Questions

1. Why is pride so dangerous (verse 23)? How can we spot it in ourselves? How can we work to prevent it (see Philippians 2:3–11)?
2. Have you ever fasted? Why/why not? Should the whole church fast before major decisions (see verse 2)?
3. How many missionaries has your church sent out? How can we encourage more short-term and long-term missionaries to go out from our congregation (verse 3)?

Acts 13:4–12

The first mission

Barnabas and Saul (who becomes Paul) set off on their missionary travels. Opposition from a false prophet is overcome and a leading citizen is converted.

Barnabas and Saul travelled the 16-mile journey west to Seleucia and from there sailed to Cyprus. Barnabas was from Cyprus (4:36) so he could show Saul around and introduce him to some of the key people on the island. They land at the major administrative centre of Salamis on the east coast and begin to preach and teach. Mark is a 'helper'; he may have carried the bags as a servant or been involved in some of the discipling of new converts – or both.

After an island-wide evangelistic tour they arrive in Paphos, the capital. Here they meet a 'Jewish sorcerer' (strictly speaking a contradiction in terms – like a 'Christian thief' – as sorcery was officially banned in Judaism) who was an attendant at the court of the island's ruler, Sergius Paulus. The proconsul wants to hear about this strange deviation from Judaism and has Barnabas and Saul brought before him. He is a wise and thoughtful man who may have had some openness to Jewish ideas. Certainly with such a large Jewish population under his authority he would have been aware of their teaching and customs.

Elymas, with his strange mixture of Jewish belief and occult involvement, tries to interrupt Saul's presentation of the gospel. Saul confronts him with a dramatic accusation about the source of his power (the devil), the wickedness of his life and the manipulative nature of his actions. God will strike him physically blind – an illustration of his spiritual blindness – for a time and Elymas is struck immediately. This incident is very similar to Philip's experience as he takes the gospel to Samaria. He encounters Simon the sorcerer and demonstrates the greater power of God (8:9f). Paul encounters Elymas the sorcerer and demonstrates the same power of God. New areas of missionary activity do seem to provoke power-encounters of this kind (cf. 16:16).

Sergius Paulus is convinced by this demonstration of spiritual authority and the quality of the teaching he hears about Jesus. Notice that he is amazed at the 'teaching', not the miracle. Signs of supernatural activity do not seem to have been uncommon in the ancient world; clear, uncompromising teaching may have been rarer! Belief in Jesus was obviously based on a rational response to a series of facts – confirmed by a miraculous sign.

Questions

1. The devil is active today (verse 10; cf. 1 Peter 5:8). How can he be recognized and defeated? Where does 'spiritual warfare' feature in our Christian lives?
2. Paul does not seem to have been polite to Elymas! Are Christians today too nice? Why are we afraid to be blunt and direct? How can we speak the truth in love?
3. Good teaching is important. What is 'good teaching' for today? How can we increase our knowledge of biblical books and Christian doctrine?

Acts 13:13–41

Paul announces the Good News

In his sermon in an Antioch synagogue Paul lays Old Testament foundations and then explains how they apply to Jesus Christ.

God's servants in the Old Testament (verses 13–25)

From Cyprus the missionary party travel north to Perga in Asia Minor. Here John Mark leaves them and returns to Jerusalem. Something serious seems to have provoked this departure. It was over 1,000 miles by land back to Jerusalem (or 600 miles by sea via Cyprus) – not a journey you would undertake without very good reason. Perhaps Mark is concerned that Saul is increasingly using his Roman name (Paul) and ministering to the Gentiles; he may have resented Paul's taking over the leadership of the group from his cousin Barnabas. Paul saw Mark's leaving as simple desertion, a dereliction of duty (15:38).

From Perga they went 100 miles north to Antioch in Pisidia where they were invited to speak in the synagogue – quite an honour for these Christian travellers. Perhaps the synagogue rulers were vaguely sympathetic, genuinely interested or just imagined Saul and Barnabas were good orthodox Jews visiting from Jerusalem! Saul stands up and begins his first recorded speech in Acts. The content of the sermon has similarities with Stephen's to the Sanhedrin (7:2–53).

Paul describes the powerful hand of God at work in one major strand of Jewish thinking – the provision of the land. This land was kept from them while they were in Egypt and while they grumbled in the desert; God kicked out the Canaanites from the land and provided a succession of judges and a king until David arrived. This man was approved by God and was the human dynasty through which God chose to reveal his Messiah. The land is important because it provides a context for the Messiah to be born into and shows God's faithfulness to what he promised, but the Messiah is the crucial part of the revelation.

Jesus is God's Messiah, the Saviour (cf. Matthew 1:21), and was introduced to the Jews through the last of the Old Testament-style prophets, John the Baptist. John is quite clear that he is not the Messiah, but with brutal honesty and a total lack of pride he explains that he is not even worthy to be Messiah's slave, the one who helps take the Master's shoes off (cf. Matthew 3:11). He, like others before him, simply points the way.

God's Son in the New Testament (verses 26–41)

Paul starts the second phase of his speech with a similar phrase to his opening; he identifies Jews and Jewish converts or God-fearers in his congregation. This section of the sermon finds echoes in Paul's letters (1 Corinthians 15:3–5) and is a repetition of some of the main features of Peter's earlier sermons, for example, Jewish leaders were responsible for Jesus' death (4:10); apostles were witnesses to the resurrection (cf. 2:32). This reminds Luke's readers of the core material at the heart of early Christian preaching and the commitment to these facts by both Peter and Paul – the two characters who emerge as the most influential in the first period of Christian development.

This similarity with Peter's material is most striking in the section which points away from David, the great Jewish hero, to his 'successor' Jesus, who has been prophetically foretold (Psalm 2:7). David stayed dead so Psalm 16:10 (quoted in verse 35) cannot apply to him, therefore it must apply to someone else. That 'someone else' is Jesus, who is not dead but alive (cf. Peter in 2:27–31 where the argument is identical).

113

Paul is impressive because he can not only articulate the historical facts clearly but he can interpret their *significance* and apply it both corporately and personally. This remarkable ability, seen supremely in Jesus (Matthew 7:29), was absent in most of the teachers of the law who knew the minutiae of the Scriptures but not what their purpose was. Paul, on the other hand, knows the content of Jewish law and history (even if he is a bit hazy about where two of his quotations come from: verse 34 – Isaiah 55:3; 35 – Psalm 16:10) and has the wisdom and divinely given insight to apply it.

The sermon ends with a gentle appeal, 'brothers', that only through Jesus can anyone be forgiven of their sins (cf. 2:38). 'Everyone who believes' is a remarkable statement to make in a Jewish synagogue; it suddenly opens up the door to the residents of a planet rather than the people of a single nation. The gentle appeal is followed up by a warning taken from Habakkuk 1:5: 'Watch out those who mock this message, they are finished. God is doing something so wonderful, so mind-blowing, you just can't comprehend it.' 'Take care' says Paul. Don't miss out on what God is doing.

Questions

1. Christians sometimes fall out! How do we treat people we have fallen out with? How can we bring about reconciliation?
2. Jews were sometimes so focused on a good thing (the land) that they missed the best thing (the Messiah). In what ways can the good things become bad, or are used for wrong purposes?
3. What do you think is the basic core-material of our faith? Which ten subjects would you cover in a discipleship course for new Christians?

Responses to the gospel

**Paul and Barnabas continue to answer
questions and present the gospel to any
who will listen. The message produces
both conversions and persecution.**

Paul and Barnabas leave the synagogue and
appear to be well received; at least people
seem open-minded enough to hear more
from them on the following Saturday. A
sizeable group seems to have been caught up in the excitement
of the message and are urged on by the two visitors to continue
being faithful to the teaching they have heard. Both the element
of human responsibility *continue* and the element of divine
activity *grace* are stressed here. Life in the kingdom is a
partnership with God. We are not free to abdicate all responsibility for our spiritual lives to God, neither are we condemned to
carry the burden alone – he provides his grace, we commit
ourselves to living in its power.

After a week of great anticipation a huge crowd gathers to
hear Paul and Barnabas. The sheer size of the crowd produces
envy in the Jewish leaders; things are getting out of hand and
they are in danger of losing their status and influence. They hurl
insults at Paul, mocking what he is teaching, and this despite
Paul's warning about such behaviour. Paul and Barnabas are
forced to respond to this attack by explaining that if they don't
want to respond to the Good News they will go direct to the
Gentiles. God has used Isaiah 49:6 to call them to the Gentiles
and they are not going to be disobedient.

These statements become the operational method for Paul and

115

his mission team – first to the Jews, then to the Gentiles (cf. Romans 1:16). He adopts this policy in all the cities he visits.

The crowd of Gentiles in Antioch were delighted and many were converted as God worked in their lives. The gospel even got out into the district around Antioch, but their success was not without cost. Civic leaders, and others in authority, were encouraged to see Paul and Barnabas as trouble makers. They were thrown out of the town and driven away from the district completely. In a typically Jewish protest – a gesture of scorn – they distanced themselves emotionally and spiritually from their persecutors. They also distanced themselves physically by travelling the 80 miles south-east to Iconium. The disciples left behind were far from discouraged – the Holy Spirit had given them a supernatural joy.

Questions

1. What happens to our Christian lives when we try to do things in our own strength? And when we don't try at all? How can we keep the balance?
2. Some groups of people are more responsive than others to the gospel. What kinds of people in your community are most open to Jesus? How can they be reached?
3. Would you have been filled with joy with all the trouble in Antioch? What produces joy like this? How is joy different from happiness?

Opponents of the gospel

As the Good News was preached in the first century world it met resistance in a number of different ways. The sophisticated intellectuals (e.g., Agrippa and the Athens Council) enjoyed discussion but shied away from personal commitment. The deeply religious Jews (e.g., 13:45; 26:22) were jealous of the Christians and unwilling to take the next step of faith – from God to Jesus, his Son.

The worldly-wise cynics (e.g., Felix) were simply not interested in *truth*, but wanted to use Christianity for their own ends. The greedy materialists were angry when their wealth was threatened (16:19; 19:25–27) and the Satan-inspired occultists (e.g., Simon and Elymas) wanted to manipulate the message and its power for their own ends.

This opposition was countered by the power of the Spirit and the teaching of the Word (e.g., 13:6–12). We face similar opposition today, but have access to the same weapons of the Word and the Spirit.

Acts 14:1–20a

Preaching provokes persecution

Teaching and miracles are followed by threats of violence. Signs and wonders then provoke hero-worship and later stoning.

The truth causes divisions (verses 1–7)

When they arrived in Iconium they made their way to the synagogue as was their habit in a new situation (cf. 13:5, 14). The Good News was so convincingly explained that a large number of both Jews and Gentiles believed. The mention of the Gentiles so early on in the ministry at Iconium is a reminder of the growing focus on them in this missionary enterprise. The Jews may be contacted first, but the Gentiles are not second in any way which diminishes their value as people or their equal right to hear and respond to the gospel.

But as usual trouble is just around the corner, following what is becoming a familiar pattern! Notice how similar Antioch and Iconium are in this respect:

▶ initial interest and response (verse 1; cf. 13:44);

▶ angry stirrers of trouble (verse 2; cf. 13:50);

▶ persecution and leaving (verses 5–6; cf. 13:50).

Despite the pressure the mission team remains in the town for 'a considerable time' – perhaps several months – preaching with courage a message which God is pleased to honour with amazing demonstrations of power. These 'signs and wonders' would probably be miracles related to sickness and releasing the demonized.

Rival viewpoints were expressed all over the city; no doubt one of the main talking points of the day was whose side you were on in the apostles versus Jews debate. Opinion was divided. The hostile element, with a little encouragement from their leaders, decided to stone them. This was not the formal punishment a synagogue might impose (cf. 7:58), more of an illegal lynch-mob involved in a deadly mugging attempt. It was time to move on. This time just 40 miles to the south-west, to a town called Lystra which was in a different district from Iconium. Far from being cowed into silence or driven underground, they continue to tell everyone the message of Good News.

These incidents in Antioch and Iconium (and there will be plenty of others throughout Asia Minor) are something of a puzzle to our western twentieth-century minds. If Paul and Barnabas spoke in Hyde Park Corner in London or Times

Square in New York it's hard to imagine any response other than some heckling; the vast majority of people would ignore them. But this was a day when what you believed was important; it would affect the way you viewed citizenship and your loyalty to the state. Beliefs were a means of political control – Christians were threatening the very fabric of ancient society.

Paul is worshipped then stoned (verses 8–20a)

Lystra was populated by a largely uneducated, rural people. There were a few Jews in the city but they seem to have had little influence. There may not even have been a synagogue so the apostolic team gets straight into street preaching, to anyone who will listen. While Paul was speaking he saw a lame man in the crowd. Luke is at pains to describe the extent of his disability, he has badly damaged feet, was born this way and has never been able to walk, in order that the amazement which follows his healing can be understood. Paul sees a rising of faith in the man and instructs him to get up and walk. He does! This story has many similarities to the healing at the Beautiful Gate (3:4–7): God's power again breaks through as the gospel is preached in a new setting.

The response is completely unexpected. Of course the people are amazed at the power working through Paul and Barnabas, but amazement was the usual response (cf. 3:10).What was not usual was for them to be thought Greek gods! In the unsophisticated, superstitious minds of these Lycaonians this was Zeus (Barnabas) and Hermes (Paul) granting them a special divine visitation. It took a while for the apostles to catch on to what was happening because the crowd had lapsed into a local dialect. And, of course, a response like this in a largely Jewish crowd, or where Jews had influence, would be unthinkable. As this was the usual scenario Paul and Barnabas were totally unprepared for what was happening.

By the time the priest of Zeus arrived with sacrificial bulls, however, they were beginning to understand. This behaviour would have been idolatrous to Jews and Christians so everything in Paul and Barnabas was repulsed by this. They ran among the people tearing their own clothes as they did so (a Jewish symbolic action showing distress or remorse: cf. Joel 2:13; 2 Kings 19:1–3) and urged them to stop. Paul's briefest recorded sermon follows: 'We are men like you, there is only one living God, he is the one who made everything and has provided rain for your crops. We are only his messengers!' The sacrifices are only just avoided.

So fickle is public opinion (if they are not gods they must be imposters!) that the Jews from Iconium and Antioch have little difficulty putting their earlier plan into action – Paul is stoned and left for dead outside the city. Incredibly he recovers and bravely returns to Lystra.

Questions

1. Some minds in this story were 'poisoned'. How does this happen today? Gossip? Slander? Deceit? Why do we find it so easy to use our tongues as a poisonous weapon (see James 3:8)?
2. Why don't we threaten the fabric of our society? Why is church life often so tame compared with the church in Acts? How would you like to have Paul as a member of your church? What difference would it make?
3. Is the superstition in this passage around today? What forms does it take?
4. Idolatry was common in the ancient world. What 'idols' do we worship today? If advertising is a guide, what kind of things do people really want?

Acts 14:20b–28

The return to Antioch

Paul and Barnabas travel to Derbe then revisit the towns in Asia Minor before returning to their base at Antioch. This completes the first missionary journey.

After being brutally attacked Paul makes an amazing recovery, so amazing that he can set off the next day and begin the 70-mile walk to Derbe. Not only was he a man whom God used powerfully, but he must also have been a strong, determined character to cope with all the physical abuse and emotional pressure he experienced on his travels.

Luke tells us about the church being established in Derbe in the briefest terms before telling us about Paul retracing his steps. He visits each of the towns where they planted churches before returning to Antioch in Syria. This seemingly simple section of Acts glides over the incredible courage of Paul and Barnabas. Just to mention the towns where they had been so badly treated, never mind revisit them, must have sent shivers down their spines! Presumably they entered each city secretly (by night? in disguise?) and limited their ministry to the believers, so minimizing the risk of detection. They were motivated in these daring visits by the needs of the new, fledgling churches which they had established. They would only survive with additional teaching and the provision of Godly leadership, elders, to guide them. These elders were appointed in a similar manner to Paul and Barnabas for their missionary work – in the context of prayer and fasting (cf. 13:2–3).

Luke records two aspects of apostolic teaching in these

situations – encouragement to persevere and a warning to expect hardship. It's hard to think of more helpful, relevant, pastoral advice. For these infant churches the Christian life is not going to be easy but it is going to be wonderful. For many modern churches it is easy but it is not very wonderful!

Journeying south from Antioch they arrive at Perga where they have the opportunity to preach, an opportunity they were not able to enjoy on their first visit (13:13–14). Eight miles away, on the coast at Attalia, they take a boat back to Antioch in Syria where they were commissioned (13:1–3). How thrilled the church must have been to have its missionaries back on furlough, telling how God had revealed himself, especially to the Gentiles. Their long stay was, no doubt, for rest and recovery (perhaps Paul needed some medical attention after the stoning) . . . not to mention being spiritually nourished themselves!

Questions

1. Notice the emphasis on follow-up in this mission. How can we best follow up our new converts? What do they need most in the early weeks?
2. It was very hard to go back to these towns. Where is the hardest place for you to be a Christian? Home? Work? How can we encourage each other to be bold?
3. Paul and Barnabas arrived safely back. How do we greet missionaries on their return? How can we let them know they are loved while they are away?

Acts 15:1–21

The Jerusalem Council

The early church is faced with deciding how much of Judaism Gentiles need to practise. Paul and Barnabas go as delegates to a council, which decides that Gentile Christians are not bound by the Jewish law.

The case for the Gentiles (verses 1–11)

Antioch in Syria receives some visitors who begin teaching that circumcision is essential for salvation. These Jewish Christians from Judea may have heard from Mark about the Gentiles coming to faith in large numbers (13:13) and were anxious to reassert the place of Judaism among all the believers. The teaching about circumcision was not simply about submitting to a physical operation, but had implications about their respect for Jewish law as a whole. Paul and Barnabas opposed this vehemently and it is obvious a major disagreement has erupted. Only a full-scale debate can settle the matter, and Paul and Barnabas are sent with a delegation to Jerusalem.

As they travelled they told what God was doing among the Gentiles (gathering support for their case?) and in the course of their 300-mile journey made many churches excited by stories of God's power. Their arrival in Jerusalem was warmly welcomed by the church, and a preliminary report of their missionary work was shared.

When the Council begins in earnest representatives of the teachers who had been in Antioch restate their position. No doubt a variety of views were expressed and then the leadership withdrew to consider the matter. 'After much (heated?) discussion' Peter stands up to make a major contribution to the debate. He argues against the 'Pharisee party' Christians (verse 5) and in favour of Paul and Barnabas. His argument is based on two principles: *his own experience* and a *theological truth* – salvation is only through Jesus.

God has already shown his commitment to the Gentiles through Peter's ministry to Cornelius (10:9–48). This incident (though perhaps ten years before) was known to everyone, and had been approved at the time (11:18). In addition, the message had always been about Jesus and turning to him as the sole provider of salvation (4:12); to add the Jewish law as a requirement would be a 'yoke' that would result in bondage. Peter ends with the clear assertion that both Jews and Gentiles are 'saved' in exactly the same way – through Jesus (John 14:6b). God does not distinguish between Jew and Gentile, shows no favouritism (10:34–35) and accepts everyone on the same basis: faith on their part (verse 9), grace on God's part (verse 11).

All nations are received (verses 12–21)

After Peter's crucial speech the assembly grows silent; the hot debate between various factions settles down, and Barnabas and Paul are allowed to share eye-witness accounts of what God is doing among the Gentiles. The Council heard how the same miraculous power which God had used to confirm his message to the Jews was also released among the Gentiles (3:2–3; cf. 14:8–10). These accounts and Peter's speech seem to have convinced the Council.

James, by now established as a key leader in the Jerusalem church and almost certainly acting as chairman of the Council, sums up the situation. Obviously whatever Peter said would be influential and James (calling him by his Hebrew name – 'Simon') affirms the pivotal significance of the Cornelius incident (9:14). In addition, he reminds the Council that the Old

Testament saw a place for the Gentiles in God's purposes. He quotes from Amos 9:11–12 to show that God had always intended there to be two distinct (but linked) groups who would share in the blessing the Messiah would bring: restored Jews, 'rebuild David's fallen tent' (verse 16), and 'Gentiles who bear my name' (verse 17).

James gives a précis of the summing up when he declares that nothing should be done to put obstacles in the way of Gentiles who want to turn to faith. They will not have to embrace Judaism; they may come to God on the same basis as the Jews (verse 19; cf. verse 11). This judgment is a clear affirmation of the ministry of Barnabas and Paul. They must have been delighted!

James goes on to suggest some practical guidelines for Gentile behaviour. These instructions seem to be given *not* to appease the Jewish faction but to ensure harmonious relationships between Jewish and Gentile groups of believers. James seems keen that the freedom from the law that Gentiles now enjoyed did not turn into licence, causing unnecessary offence to their Jewish brothers and sisters. He suggests four things which should be avoided to ensure fellowship between Gentile and Jewish Christians – three relate to food. This was a big issue for Jews and deeply embedded in their culture. What you ate and how you ate it had major ceremonial and religious implications. Jesus challenged this thinking (Matthew 15:16–20) and Peter's vision also challenges it (10:11–16).

Questions

1. What things do we add to the simple gospel message? What do people need to believe to be part of your church?
2. Is Jesus really the only way to God? What about other religions? Or being a nice person? Or doing your best?
3. In what ways do we make it difficult in our churches for those who are not Christians (see verse 19)? What do they find difficult? Our services? Our premises? Our organizations?

Acts 15:22–34

Spelling out the decision

The Council writes down the decision it has come to and sends it with a delegation to Antioch. The letter is well received and the church is encouraged.

It seemed sensible to the Council to convey their feelings on such an important matter in writing and in person. A decision of this significance must be communicated as clearly as possible. Judas and Silas are chosen as representatives of the Jerusalem church to take the letter and explain its content. The letter is intended to be read in Antioch first, but also to Gentile Christians over a much larger area – Antioch, Syria and Cilicia. This is not a small issue where a single group of believers has a problem, and the mother-church responds to it. This is the largest single issue the church has faced in its short history – every Christian congregation will be affected by the Council's decision.

The letter makes it clear that the teachers who provoked the trouble in the first place were not sent or authorized by the Jerusalem church. The letter also clearly affirms Paul and Barnabas both in themselves – 'dear friends', and in their ministries – 'risked their lives'. The decision the letter contains has a divine source combined with their human wisdom – God approves of Gentile mission and so do the Jerusalem Christians! The four guidelines to promote good relationships between Jewish and Gentile believers are spelt out. Abstain from

▶ food sacrificed to idols
▶ blood

▶ the meat of strangled animals

▶ sexual immorality.

Notice that these are issues of immense practical importance, not just theoretical niceties. For example food offered to idols was a major source of friction and disagreement at Corinth (1 Corinthians 8f).

It must not be forgotten that the Jerusalem Council has made a gracious, generous and costly decision for them. Every advance among the Gentiles makes their own situation among Orthodox Jews more difficult. By coming to this decision they have opened themselves up to the probability of ever-increasing persecution in their own country.

The church in Antioch was called together for a special meeting where the letter was read and explained. Not surprisingly, it was received with great delight. It was useful to have two such gifted brothers as Judas and Silas in Antioch, and their prophetic ministries were put to good use. There was much encouragement – both through the letter and through their ministry (verse 32). Living in this huge centre of vice and other religions they probably needed it!

Silas and Judas eventually return to Jerusalem taking happy memories and blessings back home.

Questions

1. How many of the four guidelines in verse 29 apply today? Explain your answer!
2. Right decisions can be costly decisions. Think of some examples.
3. Encouragement is vital in church life. How can we encourage . . . the lonely? the pressurized? the leaders? How can we develop a 'ministry of encouragement'?

Acts 15:35–41

The second mission

**Now that a clear position has been
established on Gentile evangelism Paul
and Barnabas are anxious to spread the
word still further – separately!**

Paul and Barnabas stayed in Antioch with a
ministry both to believers ('taught') and non-
believers ('preached') – along with an
increasing number of people who were
developing these ministries (verse 35). Paul was a man born
with 'itchy feet'! By Acts 15 he has been in Tarsus, Jerusalem,
Damascus (Arabia), Damascus, Jerusalem, Caesarea, Tarsus,
Antioch, 'the first missionary journey', Antioch, Jerusalem and
back to Antioch. He suggests to Barnabas that they need to
revisit the churches they have planted. Barnabas agrees, but
wants to take his cousin Mark with them (verse 37). It is a case of
'once bitten, twice shy' for Paul, who considers Mark a deserter
(verse 39; cf. 13:13). Paul appears to doubt his 'stickability' and
may still feel personally aggrieved by Mark's attitude.

Paul and Barnabas are unable to reconcile their differences,
have 'a sharp disagreement' and split up as a mission team. It is
helpful to realize that personality clashes and strong differences
of opinion occurred in the early church as well as today! God, in
his wisdom and power, turned this sad situation to the benefit of
the church. Now there were two mission teams instead of one!
Barnabas and Mark, and Paul and Silas set off in different
directions to preach the gospel and encourage the believers.
Barnabas and Mark went back to Cyprus, the home of Barnabas
and where the first mission had begun, and Paul and Silas

headed north, through Syria, back to Paul's home territory, Cilicia. Paul, when known as Saul, seems to have been active in Tarsus when he was sent there for his own safety from Jerusalem (9:30). Churches were obviously planted by him throughout the region surrounding Tarsus.

Silas was an excellent choice of travelling companion and co-missionary with Paul. He was evidently highly respected by the Jerusalem church (verse 22) and would help give Paul added credibility in Jewish Christian circles. He was a Roman citizen like Paul (and unlike Barnabas) which would stand him in good stead for their dealings with the authorities (16:37). He was also a prophet and Paul seems primarily to have been a teacher (see comments on 13:1). This was precisely the 'ministry mix' which had worked so well for Barnabas and Paul on the first mission. It was a team which met with the approval of the Antioch church, who gladly and prayerfully sent them out.

Questions

1. Should we only work in the church with people we like? How can we resolve personality conflicts? Are there ever 'irreconcilable differences' which would cause us to part company from our fellow workers?
2. Silas had lots of the right qualifications – both in ministry and background. What kind of qualifications should we look for in a . . . housegroup leader? steward? missionary? preacher/teacher?
3. Why do you think teachers and prophets need each other? What happens in church life when only one of these ministries is present?

Acts 16:1–15

Europe's first convert

**Timothy and Luke joined the team. God calls
them to Macedonia on the European mainland
and Lydia becomes the first European Christian.**

Obedience to cultural customs
(verses 1–5)

Back in Lystra, a town he is unlikely to
forget in a hurry (14:8–20), Paul discovers a
believer called Timothy who, with his mother Eunice (2
Timothy 1:5), was probably converted during Paul's first visit
to Lystra. Timothy was youthful (1 Timothy 4:12) yet had
already gained an excellent reputation in the churches despite
his natural reticence (perhaps even shyness? cf. 2 Timothy 1:7).
He was educated by a Greek father but thoroughly versed in
the Jewish Scriptures (2 Timothy 3:15) – no wonder Paul saw
great potential in this young man.

Paul arranged to have Timothy circumcised: verse 3 need not
mean that he wielded the knife himself! This should have
happened in infancy, but perhaps pressure from a Greek father
prevented it. Paul insists on this, as a special case, to put right an
error (culturally) which had occurred. It has nothing to do with
his Christian commitment; it simply recognizes that Jewish boys
are circumcised, so Timothy ought to be. Being a Christian did
not mean a rejection of 'Jewishness' but a rejection of Jewish law
as a means of salvation (cf. 4:12; 15:11).

So, after a few days to recover, Timothy and the missionary
team leave Lystra, taking the letter from Jerusalem and explaining its implications (verse 4). These missionary visits result in

local churches being built up spiritually and seeing growth numerically.

Obedience to God's call (verses 6–13)

The team were planning to push west into Asia, presumably to impact the major settlements of influence there, including, for example, the seven churches mentioned in Revelation 2–3. God told them not to do this, so they went north instead, hoping to minister up near the Black Sea (Bithynia). God again told them not to go, so they turned west, ending up in the Port of Troas, on the Aegean Sea. Here Paul has a vision of a man pleading with him to make the 150-mile journey across the Aegean Sea to Macedonia (verse 9). Paul responds to this 'at once', believing it to be a clear call by God to a new situation. Notice how 'they' becomes 'we' in verse 10 – Dr Luke (Colossians 4:14) seems to have joined the team, perhaps because Paul was sick?

Three times in this passage God supernaturally alters the destination of the travellers (verses 6, 7, 9). This is *his* mission: the message is about him, the Power is from him and the directions are given by him.

With favourable travelling conditions, the mission-team sails from Troas to Neapolis (via the island port of Samothrace) in two days. Neapolis was the port which served Philippi and was only ten miles away. Philippi was a Roman colony which gave it considerable independence from the regional authorities and direct access to the emperor, and Paul undoubtedly saw it as a strategic place to establish a church. There does not seem to have been a synagogue, but the citizens of Philippi do appear to be aware of a small group meeting by the river; Paul goes in search of it, and finds it just outside the city. They sit with the women and take the opportunity to talk with them about the gospel.

An opened heart and an open home (verses 14–15)

Lydia is there, a business-woman who traded in up-market

clothing ('purple cloth'); the congregation could well have been made up of business associates and members of her household staff. She already knows about God and Paul gives her the opportunity to know him personally. This affluent woman, who is 400 miles from home, is moved by what she hears and responds positively to the Good News. She and her household members are baptized – perhaps there and then in the river (cf. 8:36; 9:18). The baptism is followed by an expression of practical hospitality. The mission-team would need somewhere to stay and she appears to have a substantial property. This generous offer would be very valuable to a group of travellers with limited financial resources. In any case, ancient hotels (inns) were expensive, dirty and not always safe. On the other hand, Paul and his team could not afford to be compromised in any way. They had to be sure that this was a bona-fide offer. Once they were sure, they gladly accepted.

This is hardly a momentous start to the mission in Philippi. The contrast with some other cities, where miracles and large numbers of converts are mentioned (e.g., 14:1, 21), could hardly be more stark. The church in Philippi was started by three Jews (Paul, Silas and Timothy) and a Gentile (Luke) who had an initial congregation of one woman and her household! From this unimpressive beginning a sizeable, generous, well organized church was established (see Philippians 1:1; 4:15–16).

Questions

1. How sensitive are we to God's guidance? Paul has a vision. What methods does God use to guide? As a church? As individuals?
2. Paul and his team go looking for people to share the gospel with. How keen are we to seek out witnessing opportunities? What are the best places for you to tell others? Church? Home? Shopping? School gate? Recreation Centre?
3. Hospitality is important in church life. How many people

have we had round for coffee/dinner recently? How can we develop the gift of hospitality (1 Peter 4:9)?

Acts 16:16–40

Prison becomes a place of freedom

Paul and Silas denounce an occult fortune-teller and land in jail. Their witness is instrumental in the jailer's conversion.

Faith confronts profit (verses 16–24)

As they were going to the place of prayer by the river the missionaries were intercepted by a girl possessed by an evil spirit. She has a demonically-inspired gift of foretelling the future and seems to have done so with some accuracy, judging by the large sums of money she was making for her 'employers' (verse 16). She seems to have been drawn to the missionaries and kept yelling at the top of her voice about the fact that they were God's messengers telling about his plan of salvation. Notice a similar response to Jesus when the demon accurately identifies who he is (Mark 1:24). This is free advertising for the missionary team, but not at a time or place, or in a manner which helps them. They certainly do not want to run the risk of being associated with anything occultic.

This shrieking goes on for days and days until Paul can no longer bear to see this poor girl so dominated by the Evil one; nor does he want his lack of response to be misread as fear or powerlessness. Using the name of Jesus to full effect he casts the evil spirit out. It leaves her, she is now silent and devoid of her ability to foretell the future.

Her bosses, with no apparent concern for the girl's personal well-being, are very angry at losing such a lucrative source of income. They drag Paul and Silas into the market square and demand punishment from the magistrates. The scene in the market place is less than a riot but more than a 'scuffle' – enough for the magistrates to have a genuine fear that major public disorder could erupt. The girl's 'employers' incite the crowd by stirring up racial hatred and bigotry ('Jews' versus 'Romans') and by accusing them of encouraging Romans to break the law. The rule of law was of vital importance in the volatile cities on the edge of Europe. This accusation (and an angry mob!) panicked the magistrates into hasty, overly brutal action.

The jailer is commanded to look after them carefully: the last thing the magistrates want is an escape and another near-riot on the streets. The jailer takes no chances: he puts them in the top-security cell and secures their feet.

Joy emerges from despair (verses 25–40)

Paul and Silas must have been in some pain after their brutal flogging, but they can still find enough energy to pray together and sing out loud – at midnight! Suddenly an earthquake shakes the prison and everyone's chains fall off. The jailer knows that if a prisoner escapes he will have to take the punishment they would have had. Doubtless several of his prisoners were on 'death row', so he decides to kill himself to avoid torture and death at the hands of his superiors (verse 27). Paul assures him that no-one has escaped. The jailer calls for some light to check this for himself and discovers that it is true.

His response is amazing. He wants to know how to be 'saved'. Had he heard Paul preaching in Philippi? Was he listening in on the prayers and songs earlier in the evening? All we know is that he has concern for his soul and believes that Paul and Silas can help. Paul replies by pointing his captor to Jesus (verse 31; cf.

4:12; 8:12; 15:11). The jailer doesn't really understand the implications of this, so Paul and Silas take time to help him make an informed decision. Baptism is the next step (cf. Lydia, verse 15) followed by some basic medical attention and a little hospitality.

In the middle of all this suffering 'joy' is the overwhelming feature of this 'dead-of-the-night' scene (cf. 13:52). In Acts suffering and joy are not opposites; in fact the former seems to stimulate the latter (5:41).

At dawn the magistrates send their assistants to order the release of Paul and Silas, but Paul has other ideas. He is a Roman citizen and has rights which could not be easily trampled on. Silas shares this status, but they have both been flogged in public without a trial and imprisoned; all this is in violation of their rights as Roman citizens. Paul and Silas could have pressed charges but will settle for a little eating of 'humble-pie'. Luke records (with ill-concealed glee!) the worried magistrates scurrying to the prison to escort their 'guests' from the jail, no doubt with much apologizing. Lydia's house has become something of a base for the church, so they return there to give a report on their exciting night and to encourage the brothers to stand firm (cf. Philippians 1:27–28).

Questions

1. God defeats Satan (verse 18). What evidence is there of occult activity today? How can we help warn people of the dangers of ouija boards? Seances? Fortune-telling? etc.

2. Lydia and the jailer were baptized immediately. Why do we tend to wait? Do you think there were any babies in the jailer's household? Were they baptized?

3. What does verse 31 mean? Write out an explanation in your own words. What would you have said in answer to the jailer's question?

Acts 17:1-15

Good and bad responses to the gospel

Both at Thessalonica and Berea a positive response to Paul's preaching is followed by riots provoked by jealous Jews.

Thessalonica: Paul reasons from Scripture (verses 1-9)

All of a sudden 'we' becomes 'they' (16:40b; 17:1a). Luke no longer appears to be with the group. He may well have remained in Philippi to strengthen the new church there.

The other members of the team travel south and then west, passing through two cities (without preaching?) and ending their 100-mile journey in Thessalonica. This large city was a centre for trade and commerce, attracting a variety of nationalities, among them a sizeable Jewish population. Paul, using the same method of operation which he had begun in Antioch (13:46, 'to the Jew first'), visits the synagogue. They appear to be open to discussion and debate so Paul attends over a period of three weeks to present his case. The preaching material is familiar: 'The Messiah is Jesus, and He died and rose from the dead. All of this was seen in the Old Testament Scriptures.' Obviously Luke only gives us a summary of what Paul said; there would have been much quoting of Scripture and some debate about what those Scriptures meant.

Despite the similarity of the material there is a slightly different emphasis on the approach. There does not appear to have been a spectacular miracle to generate interest or faith. In Thessalonica, the thrust of the mission seems to be to convince 'intellectually'. Luke's use of 'reasoned', 'explaining', 'proving' and people being 'persuaded' (verses 2–4), all point to Paul's clear and thoughtful approach to his evangelistic task. Miracles were an important feature of the evangelism of the early church, but they were not the only feature! In the absence of a miracle the gospel could still be communicated effectively and receive a warm response.

As people begin to respond jealousy again rears its ugly head (verse 5; cf. 13:45). Troublemakers, who are hanging around the shopping precinct, are recruited and a mob begins a riot. They rush over to where the missionaries are staying so they can sort them out! Jason seems to have got wind of this and has hidden his guests. In the absence of Paul and Silas Jason is the next best thing. He is accused of harbouring criminals who are trying to overthrow Caesar and put a king called Jesus in his place. The officials are anxious to avoid another riot but do not seem to have enough evidence for a conviction so they let Jason and the others out on bail.

Berea: the people examine the Scriptures (verses 10–15)

Paul and Silas had to leave Thessalonica in a hurry. It may well have been a condition of Jason's bail that he evicts his house guests, probably removing them from the city. The missionary team leave at night in haste and secrecy to travel south-west to Berea, 50 miles away. Losing no time they head straight for their usual evangelistic starting point – the synagogue. Luke describes the Bereans in glowing terms, noting the stature of their characters and the serious, thoughtful way they respond to what Paul teaches.

Luke contrasts the Bereans with the Thessalonians by applauding the way the former judge Paul's words on the basis of Scripture, not on considerations of culture, politics or even economics (cf. 16:19). Many of the Jewish communities (not just in Thessalonica) seem to have little concern for 'truth'. The Christian message seems to be rejected not because it is untrue so much as because it is inconvenient! Some are jealous of the missionaries' success, others are afraid that their status in the community will be affected or are fearful of Roman reprisals. There seems to have been very little attempt to engage in serious debate about the issues.

The 'ignorant' Peter and John are flogged but not offered any serious response to their claims (4:13; 5:40). Stephen gives a massive, carefully argued speech and is offered no response but rage and stoning (7:54–58)! And so it goes on. No wonder Paul is so delighted to come across a group for whom 'truth' is so important.

The people of Berea, both Jews and Gentiles, come to faith in significant numbers. Once news of this reaches Thessalonica the Jews there sent their troublemakers to stir up trouble. The situation was serious enough to remove the prime target, Paul, but safe enough for Silas and Timothy to remain behind to strengthen the new church. They took Paul to the coast and then by boat to Athens – a sea journey of about 300 miles.

At first sight, all the opposition which the missionaries experienced seems very discouraging, but it played a vital role in the spread of the gospel. The persecution forced them from town to town across Asia and Europe taking the Good News as they went. God turned *their* problems into *his* opportunities!

Questions

1. Is becoming a Christian a matter of faith or understanding? Or both? Do you believe, then understand or understand and then believe?

2. How can we learn to see our disappointments from God's point of view? Would you have thought all this opposition was good if you were Paul?! How can we allow God to take something bad that has happened, and use it for good?

3. What does it mean to be of 'noble character' (verse 11)? Which two words would you most like used about you? Why?

Acts 17:16-34

Opportunities in Athens

Paul sees Athens in all its cosmopolitan confusion and longs to change it. He preaches to Jews and Gentiles and the Council itself. He provokes interest, but not immediate belief.

Paul among the philosophers (verses 16-21)

Athens had been the centre of the world in the centuries before Paul arrived. Art, architecture, philosophy, cultural pursuits and decadence had all characterized this influential city. By the time Paul arrived it was a shadow of its former glory, with a population not in excess of 15,000. But it retained the trappings of empire and was still a centre for the religious and philosophical viewpoints of the day. What distressed Paul so much was the idolatry everywhere. He was wanting Silas and Timothy to join him, but he cannot hold back from presenting the gospel in this confused but significant city!

His two-pronged attack takes him to the synagogue (as usual) and to the commercial district where soap-box oratory is the order of the day. He talks with anyone who will listen. Paul soon comes across the two leading ideas of the day. *Epicureans* thought gods were distant and uninterested in humans. Their goal was to achieve tranquillity by banishing fears, anxieties and particularly, concern about death. *Stoics* thought of God only in a vague sort of way, and emphasized the power of people to cope with their own lives and destiny, without divine intervention. Both groups had an 'absentee' god, so Paul is immediately in conflict with them as he presents a personal God who sent a personal Saviour who could not be defeated by death!

Of course, some thought he was just a 'babbler' and not worth listening to; while others thought that he was suggesting another god, whom they had not heard of, to add to their already extensive list! Curiosity, however, won the day and they brought him to the city council (verse 19). The council would have been responsible for issues relating to religious freedom and, given their reputations as intellectual men in the philosophical market-place of the world, they would have wanted Paul to have a fair hearing. Paul is asked to state the basic teaching he advocates, and to explain its implications.

Luke does not seem to have much time for this sort of debate. As a practical man (a doctor; Colossians 4:14) he is dismissive of the Athenian theorists who can do nothing but talk, and listen to obscure facets of philosophy or some new debating point (verse 21).

A sermon for the Council of Athens (verses 22–34)

This is a significant preaching opportunity for Paul and he appears to have prepared carefully for it. The address is different in tone and content from his earlier sermons, which drew largely on the Old Testament for their material (cf. 13:16–41). Here, too, Paul also differs most from the sermons of Peter (cf. 4:8–12).

Paul begins by affirming the Athenians. They would be glad to be thought of as 'very religious' – a tribute to their open-mindedness and intellectual tolerance. Paul had even discovered an altar to a god whose name they did not know. This was either an altar put up to a god whose existence some had heard of but no-one knew much about, certainly not its name or specific powers, or an attempt to 'cover all the options', an altar just in case there turned out to be a god they had not heard of who might not take kindly to being ignored! Paul seizes on this to provide an opening for his sermon – 'let me tell you who your unknown God is'.

The apostle cuts across all their understanding of little deities and points to God. This God made everything and certainly could not be contained in a human building (temple). He is utterly self-sufficient and in charge of the people in every country in the world. He longs for men and women to find him, and even though he is incredibly powerful and awesome, he is not difficult for humans to find. Even your own poets (Epimenides and Aratus are both quoted) point you in this direction; and since we were created by God in his image, we must not think he looks like a statue of gold or silver. The time for all that superstition is over. God calls everyone to turn back from this behaviour and get ready for the day of reckoning which is certainly coming! God has raised Jesus from the dead to prove this.

The last sentence blows them away – a physical resurrection they just can't swallow! Some jeer and mock, others defer judgment to another occasion. A very small group respond to the message, and believe. By his normal standards, the mission in Athens was a failure.

Questions

1. How many different religious viewpoints are there in your town? List them. Do any of them have any truth in them? How can we respond to this?
2. Are Christians in danger of being 'all talk' (see verse 21)? How can we make sure we are people of action, as well as talk? Why do we find talking easy and action hard?
3. Paul designed his sermon for this group specifically. What signs are there of this in the passage? How should all this affect our evangelism – as a church and as individuals?

Preaching in Acts

Acts records at least 14 sermons (or speeches) which explain the Christian message. They range from a 52-verse epic sermon by Stephen, to a one-verse statement by Paul before Festus (25:8). In each case we see how the material is tailored to fit the audience without compromising its essential truth.

Paul's preaching in Athens is an excellent example of this. There are none of the usual references to the Old Testament Scriptures or Jewish history, which these Greek leaders would have little knowledge of; instead Paul uses a familiar visual aid (17:23) and quotes from two of their poets (17:28–29). Despite the clear difference of approach the same simple response is called for, *repentance* (17:30) on the basis of the same truth, the *resurrection* of Jesus (17:31) as in previous messages!

Paul's success as a preacher can be attributed, in part, to his ability to present the message in terms his hearers can relate to (cf. 1 Corinthians 9:19–23), without diminishing its challenge or reducing its demands.

Acts 18:1–17

Patterns repeated in Corinth

The Jews make a determined effort to undermine Paul and his ministry so he concentrates on the Gentiles.

Important Corinthians are converted (verses 1–11)

Paul left Athens and made the 90-mile journey west to Corinth. The two cities could hardly have been more different: Corinth was huge with perhaps as many as a quarter of a million inhabitants and was a centre for business, trade and commerce . . . not idle philosophical speculation! The peoples of the world were represented in its population and within the city limits vice of every kind could be found.

Paul needed to provide his own board and lodgings, so went to work with a couple who had a tent-making business, Aquila and Priscilla. They were travellers themselves, thrown out of Rome by the emperor (along with many other Jews), so would have been sympathetic to Paul's need for work. They may have become Christians in Rome before coming to Corinth. They not only employed him, but found him accommodation with them. This work still gave Paul time for regular Saturday trips to the synagogue to present his message (cf. 17:2).

Silas and Timothy eventually catch up with him, probably bringing money from the Philippians (Philippians 4:14f) and this frees Paul to go back into 'full-time' preaching. The message of Jesus the Messiah produces its usual hostility from the Jews (14:2; 17:5) and in an Old Testament-style prophetic gesture Paul turns away from them to minister to the Gentiles (cf. 13:46). He moves his headquarters next door to the synagogue (a bold, if undiplomatic, move!) and continues preaching. Amazingly, the most senior figure in the synagogue is converted and – no doubt helped by the example of Crispus – many other Corinthians believe and are baptized.

Paul must have arrived in Corinth in a pretty discouraged state. Athens had been a failure and he may not have felt fully recovered from the beating in Philippi (16:23). Persecution in most of the towns he visited meant that he had to move on, but God had something different in store here. God gives Paul a vision which assures him of divine support and encourages him to be bold and fearless. This 'word' came at just the right time to prevent discouragement from spoiling his ministry. Armed with this message he stays in Corinth for eighteen months; evangelizing, and also discipling new converts.

Case dismissed! (verses 12–17)

Gallio probably became proconsul about half-way through Paul's stay in Corinth, and the Jews thought this new ruler may be sympathetic to their cause. They brought Paul to the sizeable platform, or stage area, which was elevated in the market-place in Corinth. Here the proconsul would hold court, giving his verdict on various cases. They tried to claim that Paul was advocating a religious view which had not been declared legal by Rome and so he was breaking the law. This was a serious charge and, if believed, would have severely curtailed the opportunity for Christians to preach across the Roman empire.

Paul is about to launch into his defence when Gallio (known in the ancient world for his fairness, charm and wit!) responds for him. Gallio refuses to accept the charge against Paul, believing it to be a minor squabble between various factions of Judaism. He sends them away to sort out their own problems amongst themselves. There is more than a hint in this passage that he believes they are wasting the court's time. They, and their case, are thrown out of court. Even when they turn savagely on their own leader (perhaps Sosthenes became ruler when Crispus became a Christian) Gallio refuses to be drawn into the debate. The matter is closed!

Luke portrays a rational and fair Roman legal system which would not allow itself to be embroiled in religious issues unnecessarily, nor be manipulated (by the beating of Sosthenes) into an 'anything-to-keep-the-peace' response. Gallio himself emerges from this episode with great credit. The Jews of Corinth do not. Their accusation is unfair and their methods dubious. God had promised Paul that no harm would come to him and this decision is seen as part of the fulfilment of that vision. On a larger scale, this proconsul has done the Christians a huge favour by not 'finding for the Jews'. Other Roman authorities would take note of this decision and take their cue from it. Christianity had not been banned and Gallio had demonstrated his displeasure at being bothered by such a matter. Jews in other areas would think carefully before calling in the Roman authorities in their dispute with the Christians!

Questions

1. Do you think clever, intellectual people are harder to reach with the gospel than others? What are their difficulties? How can they be overcome?
2. Should Christians ever get discouraged? What can they do about it? How can we help each other?
3. Paul was not breaking the law but Christians in some countries have to if they are to be faithful to God! Is this right or should they obey the law anyway (see 5:29)? When are we not bound by the law of the land?

Acts 18:18–28

The third mission

Paul returns to Antioch, via Ephesus, and prepares for another missionary journey. Apollos is also used powerfully by God among the Jews.

Because of Gallio's decision Paul is free to remain unhindered in Corinth. But he seems to have taken a vow of some kind (a Nazirite vow? cf. Numbers 6:1–21) which involved shaving his head and he may have wanted to return to Jerusalem to offer thanksgiving to God. Paul may have made this vow to be faithful in response to God's promise and was now wanting to offer some kind of thanksgiving in Jerusalem. He was thoroughly converted to Christianity, but was a *Jewish* Christian, whose culture still mattered a great deal to him.

He took Aquila and Priscilla with him (perhaps they paid for the trip!) and they boarded a boat at the port which served Corinth and Cenchrea, and sailed east to Ephesus. Paul visited the synagogue but could stay only briefly. He left Aquila and Priscilla in Ephesus and set off by sea to Caesarea – a journey of over 600 miles! From Caesarea he 'went up' (almost certainly this means to Jerusalem) and met with the church; after seeing the Jerusalem Christians (and giving an offering for the fulfilment of his vow?) he went back to Antioch.

After what may have been about a year in Antioch he sets off on his third missionary journey, retracing his steps of the second journey, visiting the churches and encouraging them in their faith.

Enter Apollos

Luke interrupts his account of Paul at this point by introducing us to Apollos. Apollos was a Jew from the Egyptian city of Alexandria. He was an educated man who was thoroughly familiar with Old Testament Scripture. He had obviously come across the teaching of Jesus and had responded to it as best he could. He certainly knew who Jesus was but seems not to have fully grasped all the implications of the information he had heard. Fortunately, Aquila and Priscilla were on hand to fill in the gaps in his education and experience. After a period of discipleship, he felt drawn to Achaia and ultimately found his way to Corinth (cf. 1 Corinthians 3:6). The Ephesian Christians encouraged him in this venture and he proved to be an invaluable asset to the Christians there. A brilliant orator and skilled debater he took the Jews on, on their own territory – the Old Testament Scriptures. He showed conclusively that Jesus was God's chosen Messiah.

Questions

1. Notice Paul's commitment to God's will (verse 21). How aware are we of God's purposes? How can we be more sensitive to God? How can we 'discover' his will?
2. It's easy to have incomplete knowledge. How can we make sure we grow in our knowledge? How can we encourage others to grow in their knowledge?
3. Apollos was corrected in private. What does this teach us about correction and confrontation? Why is such correction necessary?

Acts 19:1–22

Miracles and superstition in Ephesus

Paul arrives in Ephesus, the gospel spreads and many great miracles confront satanic forces. Honour comes to the name of Jesus.

Believers receive the Spirit (verses 1–10)

Paul has travelled from Antioch north and west to Galatia and Phrygia (18:23), then pushed due west to the Aegean sea port of Ephesus. He had been well received when he was last here about a year ago (18:20) and approached the city with a degree of expectation. His first task is to sort out some confusion – a dozen men seem to have heard about Jesus, even claiming the title 'disciple', but their faith seems defective. And this is a defectiveness of a totally different order from the experience of Apollos (cf. 18:25–26). Not only have they not received the Spirit, they had never heard of the Spirit! They have simply expressed repentance as taught by John the Baptist (Mark 1:4).

Paul preaches to them about the one John pointed to as God's Messiah – Jesus (John 1:29–30). Once they understood that Jesus, not John, was the focus of attention, they wished to be baptized in his name. As Paul prayed for them they were filled with the Holy Spirit, and burst out in tongues and prophetic words. This experience is similar to the one enjoyed on the first Pentecost (2:4), in Samaria (8:17) and at Caesarea (10:46). The order of events may vary – repentance, faith, water-baptism, Spirit-filling – and the 'signs' of life may vary, but all these components seem to be required for full Christian initiation.

We notice that Apollos was defective in understanding but these 'disciples' were defective in fact and focus. Apollos needed to see Jesus more clearly, these men needed to see him for the first time! We also note from this passage how clearly the Holy Spirit came. As in other places in Acts, the Spirit's coming was not without its 'signs' (e.g., 4:31; 8:18). We must be careful not to reduce his coming to a form of words or a mere ritual, however orthodox and correct the form of words may be. Form is never an adequate substitute for reality!

Paul makes regular visits to the synagogue over a period of twelve or thirteen Sabbaths, trying to persuade the Jews about Jesus and his kingdom. Some refuse to believe and begin to make life difficult for Paul and the Christians so he rents a hall from Tyrannus, a local lecturer with a fearsome reputation among his students (Tyrannus = tyrant!). For two years this ministry continues and the Good News continues to spread.

Evil is overcome in the name of the Lord Jesus (verses 11-22)

Even by Paul's usual standards (which are pretty spectacular!) this period of ministry has an amazingly large number of miraculous events. The workman's aprons he used in tent-making and the clothes he wipes off his sweat with in the heat of the day are all used to bring healing and release from demonic powers. In Ephesus this sort of thing would not be unusual, but in Paul's case the healing was not due to magic cloths or lucky aprons. The healing power lay in God himself, and the faith in Jesus of the sick person receiving the cloth or apron.

Some local Jewish exorcists thought they would add a new technique to their deliverance repertoire by using the name of Jesus. It backfired horribly on them when an evil spirit spotted the deception and said, 'Jesus and Paul I know, but who on earth are you?' (verse 15). They received a terrible beating at the hands of the demonized man . . . and presumably did not try it again.

News of this incident spread like wildfire and the name of

149

Jesus became highly honoured. People were afraid of this name *Jesus* and those who wielded its power, the Christians. This is not unlike the response to the death of Ananias and Sapphira (5:11). It brought people out of the woodwork who had not confessed their occultic involvement. They may have kept some of the literature secretly at home but now it all comes out into the open. They want to make a totally fresh start. Everything they have which has been used in an occultic way, anything which is part of their superstitious past . . . is burnt publicly. A huge sum of money goes up in flames! No wonder the gospel grew after such public testimony to its power.

After this, Paul decided that he ought to return to Jerusalem – perhaps to give a full report to the church leaders there. His long-term plan was to revisit the churches he had planted, report back to Jerusalem, then head off to Rome. He was not quite finished in Ephesus, so he sent Timothy and Erastus on ahead. They could begin the task of encouraging the churches and let them know he was coming.

Questions

1. Is the Holy Spirit real to us or a phrase we know? How can we move from knowing about God to knowing him? Should we expect any sign of his power in our lives?
2. Many Ephesians burnt their parchments. How should we separate ourselves from the wrong things in our past? For example, should we throw away 'questionable' books? Can our past have a hold on us? How should we act when we think it does?
3. Do you take the name of Jesus seriously enough (see verse 17)? Why is a casual attitude dangerous? What difference would it make to our worship if we understood the true power and honour of Jesus' name?

Acts 19:23–41

Riot!

People who profit from the worship of Artemis in Ephesus stir up a riot. Emotion takes over from reason until a senior official restores order.

Jesus versus false gods (verses 23–31)

Such is the success of Christian activity in Ephesus that the established religion comes under threat. Ephesus had long been a centre for the worship of Artemis – a many-breasted goddess of nature and fertility. With the increasing demise of Ephesus as a commercial centre it had to look to pilgrims and tourists for a larger amount of its income. Anything which threatened this would have been viewed extremely seriously. Followers of 'the Way' (verse 23; cf. verse 9) were doing precisely this!

Demetrius, a man whose living was made casting figurines of the goddess in silver, was afraid that his livelihood was being threatened. He called together his fellow workers, and others in allied trades, to discuss ways of responding to the crisis. These men are losing money, and if things continue as they are they stand to lose a good deal more. In a desperate statement he pays (unwitting) tribute to Paul's success as a missionary and the growth of the church. The result of Paul telling people about Jesus is that they see the statues which Demetrius makes as irrelevant at best and evil at worst – certainly not as gods! Two things followed from this:

- we are going to be out of a job and

- the great goddess will not be worshipped as she ought to be.

It seems fairly obvious that we are not dealing here with some pious, religious men, who have a disinterested commitment to the honour of their goddess! They are motivated by their pockets (not altogether surprisingly) but their devotion to Artemis is the pretext on which they hope to build their case against the Christians. In the ancient world it seems it was more acceptable to put a man out of work than to discredit his god!

The crowd of tradesmen soon motivate an angry mob all shrieking, 'great is Artemis of the Ephesians'. Gathering momentum, they force two of Paul's travelling companions to join them as they charge eastwards across the town to a large open-air theatre; the city assembly met here. They want to force an emergency session of the city council. Paul is keen to address the crowd (never one to miss an opportunity!) but the Christians are opposed to this and even some of the civic leaders who are sympathetic to Paul's position warn him against appearing before the crowd.

Peace is restored (verses 32–41)

In the large theatre where the crowd had assembled things were going from bad to worse. People were shouting out different things and most of them did not know what was really going on. All the majority knew was that in some way Artemis was being threatened; beyond that there was ignorance and confusion.

The Jews had certain privileges in Ephesus and would have been keen to distance themselves from the Christians in case they were accused along with them. Alexander was appointed spokesman and tried to speak to the crowd. Once they realized that he was a Jew they drowned him out with their chanting. To most Ephesians the subtle difference between Jews and Christians would count for little in this intense environment. They both had no time for idols. They were the cause of the problem, not its solution.

After two hours of this, the senior non-Roman leader in Ephesus appears – the city clerk. He reminds them that the position of Artemis in Ephesus is known everywhere, it needs no defending. Given this fact they ought not to jeopardize their standing in the world by this rash act. The tourist trade is far more likely to be damaged by rumours of civil unrest than it is by the Christians. The crowd should remember that. What's more, Gaius and Aristarchus have committed no crime; they are not guilty of robbery or blasphemy against Artemis. If anyone wants to press charges let them do it through the law courts and other matters can be brought to the regular civic assembly (which may have met as often as three times a month). Then the city clerk raises the 'Roman' dimension. The Romans were generally quite lenient on their conquered nations, but civic unrest was an unacceptable expression of public feeling. It was sometimes crushed by the Romans with terrifying ferocity. The city clerk was wanting the crowd to be clear about the possible consequences of their actions and to dissuade them from any similar action in the future.

There was no justifiable reason for the unrest; they should go home. The city clerk comes across as a brave, wise man. He refuses to be panicked or manipulated into persecuting the Christians (see comments on Gallio in 18:12–17).

Questions

1. Paul had some wise friends. Do we care enough about anybody to try to stop them doing something we think is wrong? Do we have friends like this? Where can we get them from?
2. Artemis was a false god. What are the 'false gods' in society today? How do they influence our friends and neighbours? (and us!)

3. When have we seen mob action in modern society? What are the results? How should a Christian march or gathering be different?

Acts 20:1–16

Travelling and encouraging

Paul leaves Ephesus and once again returns to the churches he has established to encourage them.

A full programme of visiting (verses 1–6)

Paul had already decided to leave Ephesus (19:21) and the riot must have confirmed that this was the right course of action. He gathered the believers together to say goodbye and to encourage them to stand firm in the Faith, then he left for Macedonia. He travelled, preached and encouraged his churches on the journey west to Greece. Luke sees these return visits to churches as 'encouragement'. Of course, a certain amount of correction, even rebuke, would have been necessary; but it is all couched in the most positive of terms. Paul's ministry is as an 'encourager' (14:22; 15:32; 16:40).

After three months in Greece he travelled back through Macedonia on land, to avoid being drowned at sea in a Jewish plot. Paul's travelling companions went on ahead to Troas, but he sailed from Philippi after the Feast of the Unleavened Bread – a trip which took over twice as long as a previous crossing (cf. 16:11–12). Paul was collecting money for the needy church in Jerusalem (1 Corinthians 16:1–4) and the men with him were representatives from the donating churches. They would accompany him to Jerusalem to present the gift on behalf of their fellow-believers. A large sum of money was being accumulated, and there would be a little more security in a larger group travelling together.

Miracle in Troas (verses 7–12)

Luke has rejoined the missionary team, probably in Philippi, and the descriptions of events involve his eye-witness observations. 'On the first day of the week' they gather to celebrate the Lord's supper. This is the first clear indication of the growing emphasis on Sunday (the resurrection day) in the Christian community. The movement away from the Sabbath to Sunday would increase rapidly as the first century moved on.

The evening meeting went on for some time, and the combination of a long sermon, lack of oxygen and fatigue caused Eutychus to fall asleep. He was sitting on a window ledge and fell to his death while asleep. Paul and the others went down the three storeys to see if he was alright (he wasn't!) and an incredible miracle occurred – he was brought back to life. After a 'midnight feast' Paul talked until dawn and then left. What an amazing night it had been! Paul's superb instruction and teaching, a communion service, fellowship over a meal and somebody raised from the dead – no wonder they went home 'greatly comforted'.

Detailed plans for travel (verses 13–16)

The group of missionaries and church representatives set sail for Assos but Paul decided to walk, perhaps to teach a little longer in Troas and enjoy some time alone with God as he walked on the coastal road from Troas to Assos. They all met up in Assos and went south, visiting various ports until they arrived at Miletus. Paul chose to miss Ephesus, probably because the riot would still be in his mind (19:23f) and because he wanted the minimum delay on his journey to Jerusalem.

Questions

___

1. Why did the Sabbath change to Sunday? How is it different? How should we celebrate Sunday? How can we help those who have to work on Sunday?
2. How can we develop encouragers in the church? Why do we have so many discouragers? How can we give some practical encouragement to our leaders?
3. Death is defeated but Eutychus would die again in the future. Why is death such an avoided subject? If Jesus has defeated death in what ways can every Christian experience an even greater miracle than Eutychus?

Acts 20:17–38
Encouraging the elders

___

Paul sends for the elders of the Ephesian church and bids them farewell with words of encouragement and challenge.

___

A reminder of what God has done (verses 17–27)

Miletus was 30 miles south of Ephesus and Paul asked the Ephesian leaders to meet him there. He seems to be filled with sadness at the thought of not seeing them again and may well have had fears for the future. He uses this occasion to review the past, describe the present and prepare them for the future. It is a sermon filled with personal passion, practical teaching and theological reflection; almost a mini-epistle!

Despite trials and opposition, Paul has humbly tried to preach the gospel in Asia. He has spoken to individuals and to crowds – Jews and Gentiles – all with the same message: turn around from wrong and believe in Jesus. Now he feels called to go back to Jerusalem, though having no idea what to expect. God has warned him not to expect an easy life so he goes to Jerusalem with his eyes wide open. But however difficult it may get, in Jerusalem or anywhere else, Paul's priority is clear. His life means nothing in itself, he has only one aim: to tell people about the wonderful grace of God. This *grace* is understood by Paul both personally and theologically. He can never get over the fact that an unworthy persecutor of the church like himself (9:1–19; cf. 1 Timothy 1:12–16) should be forgiven and entrusted with this missionary task. Nor is he unaware of God's purpose for humanity as a whole; undeserving though we are his Son has died for us, and risen again (see 2 Timothy 1:9–11).

Paul has done his duty, he has faithfully proclaimed the gospel. No-one will be able to blame him for not speaking out what he knew of God's plan and purpose.

A foretaste of what God will do (verses 28–38)

Paul encourages these church leaders to take good care of their own spiritual lives and those of the people of God given them to care for. Just as Jesus was the Good Shepherd (John 10:11), they are to be under-shepherds for the sheep Jesus gave his life for. As shepherds they must be alert for all the enemies of the sheep – people from outside the church (and, sadly, some from within it) will attempt to spoil what God has begun in Ephesus. They are to be alert boxers, never letting their guard down. Paul has given three years of his life in preparing them for this moment.

Paul sees the role of overseer as a protector against false teaching. Even the pastoral image of shepherd is used in the context of protection against wolves. Many Christians today see leaders as being available to meet *their* needs and solve *their* problems. Paul sees them protecting from attack, so the ministry of evangelism can continue. Shepherds are to feed, lead and protect the sheep . . . not to carry them!

The apostle then commits these leaders to God's grace – he is the only one who can strengthen them and keep their future secure. Then he adds a note about becoming greedy for money. Covetousness is a terribly destructive thing, especially in a leader. Paul had worked as a tent-maker (18:3) so no-one could accuse him of 'free-loading' on the church (verse 34). Another antidote for greed is to make sure that they are generous to the poor and those who cannot care for themselves. This is just what Jesus would have wanted them to do. In verse 35 Paul quotes a saying of Jesus not recorded in the Gospels. Perhaps he heard it from one of the 'twelve', when he was in Jerusalem.

When he has finished, Paul kneels in prayer with them all, brothers together in Christ. Many tears were shed on this sad day; they were losing a mentor, a brother and a friend. The parting was especially painful because they thought they would never see him again. Right until the last moment they wanted to be with Paul so they went down to the dock-side with him.

Questions

1. Paul is very aware of God's grace. What has God saved you from? What might you have become? Why is it important to be reminded of this?
2. Paul has proclaimed the whole will of God. Why do we have a tendency to emphasize only bits of it? Why is this dangerous? How can we be more 'complete' in our emphases?
3. Some teachers distort the truth. How can we know what is sound teaching? Who should we trust? How can we avoid becoming suspicious of everyone?

Acts 21:1–16

Warnings of trouble ahead

Paul's journey to Jerusalem is punctuated by scenes of warm hospitality and prophecies of disaster to come.

From Miletus to Caesarea (verses 1–9)

Leaving the Ephesian elders is a huge emotional wrench and the journey to Cos cannot have been tear-free! The ship travels south from Cos to the island of Rhodes and then on to Patara. Here they find a ship going across the Mediterranean, and board it immediately. Their route takes them east from Patara out into the Mediterranean, passing within sight of Cyprus and then on into Tyre; this 450-mile journey probably took about five days.

The ship then spent a week at Tyre unloading its cargo and taking on supplies. Paul used this opportunity to meet with local Christians. Some of them, with prophetic insight, saw what dangers lay ahead in Jerusalem. This was not news to Paul (cf. 20:23) although the prophecy may have been more specific than he had previously been aware. The prophecy obviously had a profound effect on the church in Tyre; all of them, including the women and children, went with Paul back to the boat. The prayer time on the beach had similarities with his farewell to the elders at Ephesus (cf. 20:36). He hardly knew these believers but the ties between Christians, especially in a hostile environment, can be very strong, even when there has been no time for a relationship to develop in the normal way.

The voyage continued 25 miles south to Ptolemais where a

brief meeting occurred with local Christians, then on another 30 miles down to Caesarea. Here the travelling missionary team end their travel by boat. They find accommodation with Philip the deacon-evangelist (6:5; 8:4f). Philip seems to have moved his centre of operation from Jerusalem to Caesarea. He may have been based here for as long as twenty years. Luke specifically mentions his four daughters, who had a prophetic ministry. As the ties to the male-dominated Judaism weaken a meaningful role for women becomes more and more possible. They may have chosen to remain unmarried to fulfil this prophetic calling more completely; or it may simply have been the lack of suitable believing young men in the Caesarean church (a situation not without its similarities today!). Philip's daughters would have played a part, no doubt, in his evangelistic missions and the life of the local assembly.

From Caesarea to Jerusalem (verses 10–16)

Paul, probably weary from his travels and busy schedule, takes a week or two to rest at Philip's house. He wants to arrive in Jerusalem refreshed and no doubt uses the time at Caesarea to prepare himself emotionally and spiritually as well. After a few days Agabus arrives. He has a well-known and tested prophetic ministry (cf. 11:28). On this occasion he illustrates his prophetic words with a dramatic visual aid. Using Paul's belt, he ties his own hands and feet, indicating that the owner of the belt will be bound like this in Jerusalem. The Jews will hand Paul over to the Gentile authorities.

Just as in Tyre, the disciples in Caesarea and the rest of the travelling missionaries, urged Paul not to go on to Jerusalem. They are good friends to Paul with his best interests at heart; they plead with tears that he should not place his life in jeopardy. But Paul is absolutely determined to go. He is ready not only to be arrested but, if necessary, also to die.

Paul was keen to celebrate Pentecost in Jerusalem – a significant Jewish feast with very powerful Christian memories (cf. 2:1f). He may have been driven by the desire to take the money he had collected and deliver it personally to the church in Jerusalem, but there is a greater underlying determination here. He is motivated by the Spirit (20:22) and operating under a divine compulsion. Nothing will distract him from this goal. It is all reminiscent of the experience of Jesus. He, too, knew what awaited him in Jerusalem and yet was determined to go there (Luke 9:51).

When they can all see that Paul's mind is made up they stop pleading with him and commit him into the Lord's hand. This is not a resigned fatalism but a positive affirmation of what they see as God's will in this situation: humanly speaking he should not go to Jerusalem, but the Lord wills that he should (cf. Jesus in Matthew 26:39b).

Together they travel the 65 miles to Jerusalem where they are given hospitality by Mnason, one of the earliest converts. The third missionary journey has been completed and Paul is back where he feels compelled to be.

Questions

1. Philip's four daughters obviously had a valuable ministry. Do women play a significant role in church life today? How can they be encouraged? Why should they be?

2. What is the difference between determination (verse 14) and stubbornness? How can we tell the difference? Do we really *listen* to those who advise us?

3. 'The Holy Spirit says.' List the ways in which God speaks to us today. How can we recognize his voice? What role do church leaders have in this?

Acts 21:17–40

A double welcome in Jerusalem!

In the fellowship of the church, Paul reports what God has done among the Gentiles. A week later there is a riot and Paul is arrested by the Roman authorities.

Telling what God has done (verses 17–26)

As on Paul's last visit to Jerusalem (15:4), he was warmly welcomed by the local Christians. After this initial welcome, perhaps at Mnason's house, a meeting was arranged for the following day. James, the leading figure in the Jerusalem church, along with all the elders, gathered to hear a detailed report of Paul's ministry among the Gentiles. They were thrilled to hear of all the miraculous events, conversions and churches being planted; but they did have a problem.

Thousands of Jews had been converted in Jerusalem and surrounding areas – most of them keen to retain their Jewishness. Some of them had heard a rumour that Paul was encouraging Jews to turn their backs on their heritage. Gossip and rumour were rife in the ancient world (have things changed?) and it is not difficult to see how this sort of impression could be created by reports of Paul's ministry in Asia and Europe, despite the fact, for example, that he had had Timothy circumcised (16:3).

The Jewish leaders suggested that Paul 'sponsor' four poor Christian Jews who wished to undertake a Nazirite vow, as he himself had done some years earlier (18:18). This will involve him in certain purification rites himself, but also be seen as a pro-

Jewish act of kindness. This will demonstrate that Paul continues to see himself as a Jew *and* a Christian; he will show that he is committed to the gospel, but not therefore opposed to Jewish culture and tradition. Paul, wishing to correct the misunderstanding, is happy to comply with their request. The Jewish Christian leaders, for their part, are anxious to confirm that the agreed requirement for Gentiles (verse 25; cf. 15:29) still stands – they are not bound by Jewish law.

The very next day (Paul loses no time as this is only his third day in Jerusalem) he goes to the temple with the four men and begins the task of purifying himself and them. He then informs the temple authorities of the date the purification will end and that he will provide an offering for them at that time. Paul is very keen to send out the right signals to the Jewish Christians. He would never compromise on the issue of obedience to the law (cf. Galatians 2:11f) but he did not wish to deny his Jewishness, nor cause unnecessary offence to his fellow Jewish believers.

Paul under arrest (verses 27–36)

When he is almost at the end of his period of purification Paul is spotted in the temple by some Jews from Asia, perhaps Ephesus. They recognize him as the cause of much tension in Asia and seize the opportunity to stir up the crowd against him. Religious zeal is at fever pitch and the temple would be packed with pilgrims because of the Feast of Pentecost. They accuse Paul of speaking against two of the pillars of Judaism – the law and the temple. To this half-truth they add a straightforward lie for good measure. They say that Paul has brought Trophimus, the representative of the church at Ephesus (20:4), beyond the court of the Gentiles into the inner court where only Jews were allowed.

Luke explains that the only ground for saying this is that they had seen Paul and Trophimus together in the city earlier. Paul knew that the punishment for this was death, and he is hardly likely to encourage persecution when he can get plenty of it without trying! Such is the religious hysteria, however, that minor considerations (like the truth!) are swept away in the mob violence which follows. Paul is dragged to the outer courts, the inner gates are closed to prevent defilement from any bloodshed and the crowd begin to beat Paul to death.

Once news of the riot reached the Roman authorities the commander mobilizes his soldiers. He dispatches some officers and their men from the fortress of Antonia (to the north of the temple) to pull Paul out of the crowd. He is promptly arrested and dragged off back to the fortress for interrogation. Try as he might, the commander could not get any sense out of the crowd. People were shouting conflicting things and this, combined with the sheer volume of noise and the continuing violence, make it impossible to get at the truth.

The commander is determined to find out the facts and has Paul half-dragged, half-carried away from the temple and back to the relative calm of the fortress. The crowd follow them, screaming out 'away with him'. Judging by what they meant when they said the same thing about Jesus (Luke 23:18) this amounts to a demand for Paul's execution!

Paul claims his Jewish rights (verses 37–40)

As Paul is being pulled up the steps into the fortress he asks the commander a question in Greek. The commander would have been surprised to be addressed in the usual language of the Roman Empire by someone he thought was an ignorant rabble-rouser from Egypt. Three years earlier an Egyptian had gathered 4,000 men on the Mount of Olives, hoping for an opportunity to overthrow Roman rule in Palestine. They were defeated by the Roman army, but it was a serious enough uprising for the commander to remember it . . . and not want it repeated.

Paul tells the commander that he is a Jew from a significant and influential city, Tarsus. He then asks if he may speak to the crowd. This request is granted because the commander hopes to discover what the problem is between Paul and the crowd; he may also have been more kindly disposed towards Paul because of his Greek language skills and his general manner in such trying circumstances. Paul asks for silence and begins to speak in Aramaic, the local language. This surprises the crowd and wins him a marginally more sympathetic hearing.

Questions

1. Do you have to be part of English-speaking middle-class culture to be a Christian? In what ways do we force people to accept our culture with our Christ, when they come to church? How has this tension been seen in our missionary work?
2. Why do people believe lies so easily? Why is telling the truth so important? Is exaggeration a lie? Or is not saying anything?
3. Religious fanaticism continues today. Why do so many bad things happen in the name of religion? Why is religious hatred often so intense? What causes this blind devotion?

Acts 22:1–21

Paul addresses the crowd

**Paul's defence begins with his credentials as
a Jew and his persecution of the Christians.
He describes his conversion to Christ
and his call to preach to the Gentiles.**

Paul's credentials (verses 1–5)

The speech in his own defence begins as
Stephen's speech did (7:2) with a respectful,
and yet warm, greeting. It is delivered to an almost exclusively
Jewish audience. Paul explains that he was born a Jew and had a
Jewish upbringing; that he had studied with the almost
legendary Gamaliel (cf. 5:34) and had completed his training in
Jewish law. He was extremely 'zealous' in his Jewish faith. Not
only that, he put his commitment into action against the
followers of 'the Way' (9:2; 19:9). Neither men nor women had
any mercy from him so zealous was he to uphold the law.

And all these facts can be born out by the Council, who both
authorized and approved these actions. Paul even cites the High
Priest as someone who could testify to the truth of what he is
saying. He had even pursued the Christians beyond Jerusalem,
obtaining special permission to hunt them down in Damascus.

This is an impressive set of credentials. The crowd would be
totally in agreement so far . . . but the speech isn't over yet!

Paul's conversion (verses 6–16)

After establishing his thoroughly Jewish background Paul
proceeds to describe his encounter on the Damascus road

(cf. 9:3–19). This account is very close to the original story earlier in Acts, but with the distinctly Jewish elements high-lighted. Paul is accurately describing what happened to him, but placing the emphasis on certain things in order to communicate most effectively to this specific audience (e.g., Ananias is described as being a 'devout observer of the law and highly respected by all the Jews' (verse 12); and 'The God of our fathers' and 'the Righteous One' (verse 14) are distinctly Jewish phrases).

So Paul describes what happened to him on the journey from Jerusalem to Damascus. He is

- blinded (verse 6)

- confronted (verse 7)

- chosen (verse 14)

- called (verse 15) and

- baptized (verse 16)!

This dramatic story would have had the crowd reeling as each new development was unfolded before them. It is a story of miraculous events, supernatural voices and stunning words. The account of a life turned upside down. Paul is at his passionate best as he recalls that amazing day all those years ago.

Paul's commission (verses 17–21)

On his return to Jerusalem he describes a visit to the temple (notice the continuing 'Jewish' emphasis) where he had a supernatural visit from Jesus telling him to leave Jerusalem quickly because his message would provoke unrest (cf. 9:29–30). Paul was acutely aware of his reputation as a persecutor of Christians and believes it will be difficult to find acceptance among them. After all (and here Paul re-emphasizes the strength of his earlier Jewish convictions) he has hunted the Christians down; had them imprisoned and beaten; and was even party to the murder of deacon Stephen.

Despite all this, Paul is accepted by God, and the Christian community (cf. 9:26–27) and commissioned to take the message 'far away to the Gentiles' (cf. 9:15). The Gentiles were far away in two senses: Paul would have to travel many miles from Jerusalem to fulfil this commission, and the Gentiles were not 'near' to an understanding of God and his ways as the Jews were (cf. 2:39).

Paul never got complacent about the sinfulness of his past and was forever grateful for the grace of God in forgiving, and then commissioning him to such a great task!

Questions

1. Paul's upbringing was important to him. What does this imply for Christian parents? Children's work in church? Child evangelism?
2. Do you have a dramatic conversion story? Do you need one? Which facts are more important than *when* you were converted?
3. Do you have a difficult past? How can you be free from it? Is anything too bad for God to forgive? Can we start again?

Acts 22:22 – 23:10

Paul the Roman citizen

The crowd interrupt Paul and demand his death. To prevent a flogging he claims that he is a Roman citizen. A hearing is arranged before the Sanhedrin. They are divided and cannot agree a verdict.

Paul claims his Roman rights (verses 22–30)

The crowd had listened with approval to Paul's account of his Jewish background and with interest to his amazing conversion story, but his remarks about being called to the Gentiles make their blood boil. To claim that Jews and Gentiles could have access to God on an equal basis was more than they could stomach. They break into his speech, demanding his death (again! cf. 21:36), claiming he is not fit to live. They make their point in a typically Eastern manner by stripping off for action and throwing dust and dirt into the air – and the commander obviously fears a riot of major proportions. Paul is whisked inside the fortress and prepared for questioning.

The commander can not understand what the crowd are yelling, nor can he have understood Paul's defence in Aramaic. He is beginning to lose patience with the whole business. He orders Paul to be brutally flogged in order to extract a confession. This is quite different from the beating he received, for example, at Philippi (16:23). The scourge was an instrument of torture, which could cripple for life or even kill. It is not the simple whip or rod of Paul's earlier experiences. The time for gentle enquiry is over!

Just before this potentially life-threatening beating takes place, Paul announces that he is a Roman citizen. This sends the centurion scurrying to the commander and the commander back to Paul to confirm the truth of his claim. Roman citizenship was an honour shared by a privileged group; even a Roman commander had no automatic right to it. This commander had paid a huge sum of money to obtain this privilege, but Paul is able to boast that he was born into the privileged position. This puts an entirely different complexion on things. The torturers quickly disappear and the commander is relieved that he found out in time. To put a Roman citizen in chains was bad enough, but to have had him flogged would have been a very serious offence indeed.

Paul was kept in custody overnight, presumably for his own safety, and brought to appear before the Jewish council. No doubt the commander believed that it was primarily a religious question, so he ordered the highest authority on religious matters to meet and give Paul a hearing.

Paul confuses the Sanhedrin (verses 1–10)

Paul begins his statement to the Council with a description of his conscience – it is clear (cf. 20:26). Paul simply means this to be taken at face value; he has not wilfully done anything he knew to be wrong. The high priest believes it to be an arrogant claim and instructs Paul to be hit in the face by those nearest to him. The action is in direct violation of Jewish legal procedure (where a man was innocent until proved guilty) and makes Paul very angry. He calls the action hypocritical and he insults the high priest with a familiar term of abuse – 'You are a poor excuse for a wall. A rotten, broken down pile of bricks disguised to look like a decent wall with a thin coat of paint!' (Paul spoke more accurately than he knew. Ananias was a corrupt and greedy collaborator with the Romans. He stole from the priests, gave bribes and was open to them. He eventually died at the hands of his own people. God did judge him!)

The Council is amazed at Paul's language to the high priest – they are all terrified by the wealthy and influential Ananias. Paul apologizes immediately (quoting Exodus 22:28), wanting to honour the office of high priest, if not Ananias the man. As Paul is regaining his composure he remembers the natural divisions which exist on the Council and decides to exploit them. He may well have given up any hope of a fair hearing after the action of Ananias and, anyway, the Sanhedrin did not exactly have a good track record when it came to dealing with Christians (4:5f; 5:40; 7:54f). He may well be trying to avoid similar treatment to that received by the early apostles, rather than giving a reasoned defence.

He claims to be on trial for his beliefs as a Pharisee, particularly the resurrection of the dead, and this sets the Council in uproar. The Sadducees are against him and the Pharisees for him. 'Who are we to judge this man if God has spoken to him', the Pharisees argued. All the old prejudices rise to the surface and the Sanhedrin is split on party lines, with more than verbal abuse being thrown! The commander fears for Paul's safety and breaks up the meeting by force, taking Paul to the safety of the fortress.

Questions

1. Did Paul lose his temper? Was he wrong to do so? Should we ever lose our temper? What should we do when it happens (see verse 5)?
2. Did Paul tell the truth when he divided the Council or was it just a clever trick? Is it ever right to lie? In what circumstances? Should Paul be praised or condemned for this tactic?
3. Paul was a Roman citizen (verse 25). Does your citizenship give you any advantages when presenting the gospel? How has your country helped your life as a Christian? How has it hindered?

Acts 23:11–35

From danger into danger

A plot to kill Paul is uncovered. The Roman commander sends Paul to Governor Felix in Caesarea, where he awaits trial.

Escape from conspiracy (verses 11–22)

Paul, now back in his cell, may have been feeling fairly despondent after the troubles of the last few days. At this moment his Lord appears to him with a message of reassurance and hope. His longing to preach in the empire's capital (cf. 19:21) would be fulfilled! Paul must have rested more easily, and with a lighter spirit, after this Divine encouragement.

He may not have been quite so relaxed had he known what was being planned by forty fanatical Jews who had taken an oath to neither eat nor drink until Paul was dead! It confirms our fears about the corruption in high places, when we learn that this gang has no qualms about telling the chief priests about their plot and even asking for their help. Ananias and his cronies have no scruples when it comes to protecting their own interests. But Paul's nephew finds out about the plot and visits Paul to tell him. (Paul is under the equivalent of house arrest. He is not free to leave, but he could have visitors and would have been reasonably well cared for.) Paul asks that his nephew be granted an interview with the commander and a confidential discussion takes place.

Somehow Paul's nephew has acquired detailed information about the plot. Was his father invited to join the forty men? Local gossip? Is he a servant to the Jewish 'elder' (verse 14)? He describes it all to the commander who takes it very seriously. Even though he is only a boy (early teens?) his story has the ring of truth and there seems no obvious reason for making it up. Besides the commander is aware of the current Jewish mood and the character of Ananias. This plot is not unlikely.

The experienced Roman commander wishes this private conversation to remain confidential, so he cautions the teenager to tell no-one about the visit.

Jesus has promised Paul that he is going to Rome and this incident shows Jesus fulfilling his word. A human agent discovers the plot, but we can hardly fail to see a divine hand behind it. It takes nearly three years for Paul to get to Rome – through many crises – but God is faithful to his word.

Paul at Caesarea (verses 23–35)

The commander loses no time in responding to the warning from Paul's nephew. That very day he arranges an escort to take Paul to the Governor in Caesarea. The size of the escort underlines the gravity of the situation as far as Claudius Lysias, the commander, is concerned. Nearly 500 soldiers – 200 infantry, 70 cavalry and 200 light-infantry ('spearmen') in all! – take Paul by night to Antipatris, a town 35 miles away in the Judean hills. Paul is provided with a horse to ride and a horse or mule for his belongings. The foot soldiers return to Jerusalem the next day and the cavalry escort Paul the final 30 miles into Caesarea.

The covering letter explains to Felix the situation and the need for the heavily armed escort. The gist of the letter accurately conveys what has happened and why Lysias is sending Paul to Felix. However, it is hard not to find aspects of the letter amusing; it seems unlikely that Paul would have felt 'rescued' by a Roman commander who did not actually find out about Paul's citizenship until much later in the day (verse 27; cf. 21:33; 22:26). The absence of any mention of Paul in chains or the narrowly-avoided flogging of a Roman citizen indicate a certain selective memory loss on the part of the Jerusalem commander! The whole process seems to be a buck-passing exercise. Claudius Lysias cannot discover the root of the problem and certainly does not want a Roman citizen assassinated while in his custody. 'Let's get governor Felix to sort it out.'

This self-congratulatory letter was handed to Felix by a cavalry officer and Paul was transferred into the custody of the governor of Judea. Felix asks Paul where he is from: if he was from another governor's district or subject to another local authority Felix may wish to refer him to them (cf. Pontius Pilate in a similar situation with Jesus: Luke 23:6–7). When he discovers that Paul is from a Roman province, Cilicia, he feels able to deal with the situation himself. When his accusers arrive from Jerusalem Paul's case can be heard. In the meantime, a cell in what was Herod's palace will be his home. Paul would be safe and not uncomfortable, being treated with a measure of care and respect.

Questions

1. Here is a brave, responsible teenager. Was he a 'typical' first-century teenager? Why are modern teenagers so heavily criticized? What is your church doing to help them? How are their gifts being used?
2. Is the letter from Lysias entirely truthful? Is it legitimate to paint ourselves in a good light? On an application form? In an interview? At what point does this become dishonest?
3. Was Lysias evading his responsibility by sending Paul to Felix? In what ways do Christians 'pass the buck' instead of accepting responsibility (e.g., 'it's the leaders' fault')? Why do Christians find it so hard to say – 'it was my fault'?

Acts 24:1–27

Trial at Caesarea

After a brief wait in Caesarea, Paul and his accusers are brought face to face. Luke reports both sides of the case.

The case for the prosecution (verses 1–9)

As soon as he possibly can Ananias arrives in Caesarea to finish the job he wanted done in Jerusalem. The Council had failed to make the 'right' decision (cf. 23:9) and the plot to kill Paul had been thwarted (23:23). Ananias is hoping this will be third time lucky and he has come to court in person, hoping to guarantee the outcome. He has with him some of his colleagues from the Jewish eldership and a skilled legal expert called Tertullus. Ananias must have been pretty confident in his team, particularly given the reputation of Felix as a greedy, praise-hungry man, not averse to being bribed (see verse 26). Here was a kindred spirit for Ananias – a man he could do business with!

Paul is called into the courtroom and Tertullus is given permission to present the case for the prosecution. What follows is a fawning hymn of praise to Felix; even by the standards of the ancient world, where flattering rulers was the usual practice, this is 'over-the-top' crawling. Felix was a cruel butcher who had put down Jewish uprisings with brutal ferocity. Hardly a single Jew would have agreed with Tertullus' description of Judea under Felix and even less would have had 'profound gratitude'! Tertullus moves on from appealing to Felix's vanity to present the charges against Paul.

175

There seem to be three specific charges:

- he causes riots among Jews wherever he goes;

- he is ringleader of a troublesome sect;

- he tried to bring a Gentile into the forbidden part of the temple.

The basic thrust of the charges is that the 'Roman peace' is being threatened by Paul, who is a political agitator. Felix has crucified those guilty of this in the past and Tertullus is hoping for a similar verdict. Felix will find all this is true when he interviews Paul for himself, Tertullus concludes.

This is a remarkably brief speech, even briefer than Tertullus promised, so presumably Luke has only given us an outline of the main points. However long the speech actually was the Jews certainly liked it and added their own murmurings of approval and agreement. These Jews may have come from Jerusalem with the main accusers or they might be Caesarean Jews who had been 'encouraged' (bribed!) to be present in court, to support the charges.

Paul defends himself (verses 10–21)

Rather than cross-examine Paul Felix gives the apostle the opportunity to make a speech in his own defence. Paul begins by affirming the value of Felix's long association with the region (about ten years) and how glad he is to speak in front of someone who is not a stranger to Jewish practices and belief. This is a polite, positive and honest opening to his speech which must have contrasted sharply in the eyes of the court with the flowery, insincere praise of Tertullus.

Paul quickly dismisses the three charges against him. It is less than a fortnight since all this happened and he had only just arrived in Jerusalem, hardly enough time to organize a revolt of some kind. He was not the 'ringleader' of anything. He was worshipping alone in the temple, peacefully and without any attempt to incite anyone. As for the charge about desecrating the temple it simply is not true, so they obviously cannot prove what they are saying. Paul admits his background as a Pharisee, and draws the court's attention to areas of agreement between himself and his accusers. He does not deny that he is a follower of 'the Way'. Believing in a resurrection, he tries to live his life with a clear conscience knowing that one day he will face God (cf. 23:1).

The point of Paul's defence is to describe the issues in religious, rather than in political terms. He is not dangerous to the Roman empire, seeking to overthrow any institution by force or intrigue. He is in conflict with his fellow Jews about matters of religious faith and practice, and even in the conflict there are some areas of common understanding.

Paul goes on to spell out in detail why he had come to Jerusalem. His purpose was twofold:

- to bring money he had been collecting in Asia and Europe for the poor;
- to bring offerings for himself to worship at the Feast of Pentecost.

He repeats his innocence of the charges by asserting that his religious preparation was complete and that his worship was not causing any commotion. Religious and political offence was avoided by his behaviour. His real accusers are absent from the trial, the Asian Jews who stirred up the trouble in the first place (cf. 21:27), no doubt because they had nothing that would stand up in court! The Sanhedrin could not find him guilty of a crime and neither will the court of Felix – unless believing in the resurrection is a crime.

A long adjournment (verses 22–27)

Because of the link Felix has had with Judea over a number of years he has come across followers of 'the Way' before and at least has passing knowledge of some of the issues involved. He fobs off Ananias and his team with a lame excuse about waiting for the Roman commander to come and give evidence, but already he has a written statement from Lysias (cf. 23:26–30). The fact is he knows Paul is innocent but does not want to offend the Jews. He is stalling for time. At least Paul is looked after well during his period of detention.

Drusilla was Felix's third wife. He had lured her away from her husband, a Syrian king, with promises of wealth and power. He was attracted by her youthful beauty. The relationship was built on his lust and her greed. Perhaps because of Drusilla's Jewish background they arranged to hear Paul for themselves, privately. Paul spoke freely about Jesus and about faith in him. No doubt this involved his personal testimony and the presentation of supporting evidence from the Old Testament Scriptures. Paul, however, was keen to press home the lifestyle implications of the Christian faith. The three areas he touched on must have made them squirm: neither had behaved with *righteousness*. *Self-control* was not exactly Felix's strong point . . . so no wonder they feared *the judgment to come* (verse 25). This was not the sort of talk they were expecting and they found it all a bit frightening. Paul is quickly dismissed and, as far as we know, Drusilla never hears him again. Felix will hear Paul again when he has had a chance to push some of the more challenging aspects of his teaching to the back of his mind!

Felix is caught between his fear and his greed. He finds what Paul says unsettling but he hopes for a sizeable bribe to set him free. Perhaps he thought Paul had wealthy connections or that his friends might raise the money. Certainly the thought that Paul would consider a bribe morally wrong, would not have occurred to this covetous, manipulative governor!

Felix eventually goes too far in brutal excess when he viciously stamps out a problem between Jews and Greeks in Caesarea, largely by killing lots of Jews. He is recalled to Rome. For two years Paul has been waiting for a verdict – perhaps the new governor will give one.

Questions

1. Is flattery a sin? In what situations are we tempted to do it? What does it say about us? What does it say about the person we flatter?
2. They called Christians a 'sect' (verse 14). What is a sect? Who are the sects today? What kind of things do they believe?
3. 'Bribes' are still common in some parts of the world. How would you react if you had to bribe an attendant for a place to park your car or to get a parcel from home out of storage? Would you pay? Is bribery always wrong in a country where there are low wages?

Acts 25:1–11

Paul appeals to Caesar

The new governor arrives and is made aware of Paul's situation. A new trial is arranged and the same issues arise. Paul appeals directly to Caesar.

After taking only three days to settle in Festus makes his way to Jerusalem to meet the Jewish leaders. Felix has left a legacy of distrust and disharmony in Judea and Festus is keen to make a start in restoring goodwill. Festus seems to have been an excellent governor, much better than Felix, or those who followed him in the office of governor. Sadly, he died after only two years in office. No sooner had he met the senior Jewish leaders than they outline the case against Paul. Hoping to take advantage of the new governor's innocence they ask for Paul to be brought back to Jerusalem – hoping to have him assassinated en route; they had tried this same technique over two years earlier (23:12)! Festus thwarts this plan, probably quite by accident, by insisting that the trial is held in Caesarea. Paul is already there, Festus must have been anxious to get his governorship established in Caesarea and the leaders can travel back with Festus and his advisers.

Paul begins another speech of defence (verses 6–11)

After a little more than a week, the group make their way down to the coast to the Roman capital of Judea, the court is convened and Paul is brought in. The Jews repeat the same old charges and Luke reminds us that although these charges are serious they have no proof. They did not have any proof in the trial before Felix (24:13) and the last two years have not produced any either. Paul replies that he is innocent – he is not in breach of Jewish law, did not desecrate the temple and has not broken Roman law. Stalemate! We are back to square one. Festus can see no way of resolving this so he asks if Paul will go to Jerusalem to face the charges. Paul is much more aware of the Jewish tactics than Festus and knows his life would be in danger. What is more his experience over the last few years causes him to have more faith in Roman justice than Jewish injustice – where he is now, 'Caesar's court', is where he wants to be tried (cf. 18:12–16). Both Paul and Festus know that Paul is innocent of the charges but both also know it would be political suicide to free someone so hated by the Jewish establishment. Paul bails them both out of a tricky situation by appealing to Caesar.

Questions

1. Festus is an improvement on Felix. What do you think made him a better governor? What characteristics should we see in our political leaders? What standards should they live by?
2. God ensures Paul's safety. What evidence is there that God has over-ruled in your life? Looking back, can you think of cases where God was at work and you were not aware of it? Can God use non-Christians to get his will done?
3. Paul stands up for his rights. Would it not have been more Christian to agree to Festus' request? When is it wrong to turn the other cheek? What kinds of issues should we stand up and fight for?

Acts 25:12-27

The governor, the king and the missionary

Festus agrees to send Paul to Rome. King Agrippa is visiting Festus and they discuss Paul's case. Agrippa asks to hear Paul first-hand.

Festus tells his story (verses 12–22)

Festus meets with his advisers to discuss Paul's appeal to Caesar: as a Roman citizen Paul had a right of appeal direct to the emperor. This right could be exercised if a Roman citizen was on a charge for which the death penalty might be appropriate. The charge of political revolt which the Jews claimed about Paul could be punishable by death in a Roman court so his appeal to Caesar would have to be allowed.

When a neighbouring king came with his sister to greet the new governor, Festus thought it would be good to enlist his help with Paul. (What on earth would he write in his report to the emperor?) Agrippa was known as an expert in Jewish matters, so Festus picks his brains about the problem which Felix had left him to resolve.

Festus gives a fair summary of the situation, confessing freely his confusion and his surprise at the nature of the charges. They appear to him to be totally concerned with religious matters and he cannot see any reason why Paul has to be tried by a Roman court. He offered Paul the chance to appear before the Sanhedrin in Jerusalem and he declined, choosing rather to take his case to Rome. Festus informs Agrippa that Paul will be held in Caesarea until arrangements can be made to send him to Rome. This could take months to plan – Festus would have to write a report, documentation for travel prepared, a route to Rome worked out, financial arrangements made, etc. It was a journey of about 1,800 miles. No small trip in the ancient world!

Agrippa is fascinated by this case and asks to meet Paul and hear his side of the story. Festus promises to make this happen on the following day.

Festus' report to Agrippa contains a vitally important phrase which sums up the nub of the issue perfectly – it is '. . . about a dead man named Jesus whom Paul claimed was alive' (verse 19). The resurrection of Jesus was at the heart of apostolic preaching (cf. 2:31; 3:15; 4:10; 5:30; 10:40; 13:37, etc.); and was not simply an abstract theory – the first apostles had seen him (2:32) and so had Paul (1 Corinthians 15:8) – but a living personal experience. Jesus is alive!

Festus presents his prisoner to the king (verses 23–27)

Paul could not have arranged a better evangelistic opportunity if he had tried! Festus arranged for all the local dignitaries and the senior military personnel in the area to join him for a glittering social occasion. They process in, wearing their fine robes and dress uniforms, amid much pomp and ceremony. Agrippa and Bernice are the guests of honour and once they have been seated Paul is brought to stand before the group.

Festus gets proceedings under way by explaining why he has called everyone together. It all revolves around Paul. Paul must have looked out of place in the opulent arena. He probably felt fairly isolated – a Daniel in a den of Romans – yet he controls all the proceedings by his presence. In God's eyes, everyone else was out of place; Paul was in the centre of his will. The Jews have petitioned Festus, both here in the capital and in the holy city of Jerusalem, to have Paul executed. Festus does not believe that the charges hold water but, anyway, Paul has appealed to the emperor (verse 25) so Festus has no choice but send him to Rome.

But what can he say to the emperor about the case? He may

not have wanted to admit that he was appeasing the Jewish leaders, so could not let Paul go. A charge of religious controversy (within Judaism) would be dismissed by the Imperial Court as outside its brief and a charge of political sedition was unproved. Festus knew this (25:10; cf. verse 25). What was he to say? With this dilemma in mind he has called the group together to discover a way forward. He can hardly send a prisoner all the way to Rome without some kind of letter of explanation.

This is a remarkably frank speech from a new governor – very open and honest. He is not afraid to ask for their help nor confess his own weakness. Through it all Luke sees the hand of God moving clearly and certainly toward the fulfilment of his promise to Paul (23:11).

Through all the human confusion God is working his purpose out. Festus thinks he is the one sending Paul to Rome, but a larger plan than the governor of Judea knows about is being put into operation!

Questions

1. Festus admits to not knowing what to do. How ready are we to admit our weaknesses? Why do we pretend not to have problems? How can we recognize pride in our lives?
2. Jesus is alive! How do you know this is true? What evidence is there? Why is it important that Jesus did not stay dead? Do you think Christians have got blasé about this truth?
3. Festus wants to please the Jews or he would release Paul. Is it possible to want to please people too much? Or please the wrong people? Or please people more than please God? What dangers are there here?

Acts 26:1–23

Paul tells his story again

Seizing another chance to witness to his experience of God Paul begins with his orthodox Jewish past, then describes the incident on the Damascus road and how he has put into practice what he was told to do.

The Jewish background (verses 1–11)

Festus hands chairmanship of the occasion over to Agrippa who invites Paul to speak. With an orator's gesture of respect for the chairman Paul begins. It was the custom to begin such occasions with words of affirmation (cf. 24:2–3) and Paul offers his sincere appreciation for Agrippa's grasp on Jewish issues. He is pleased to be able to address such a distinguished group and delighted that its chairman has such a long family association with the Jews. He asks for patience so he can deliver an extended explanation.

Paul was brought up as a Jew in Tarsus and Jerusalem, all the Jews can testify to this. He became a Pharisee and was known for his strict adherence to the letter of the law. All Pharisees live in the expectation of the resurrection which was promised us by God, generations ago. The whole nation is desperate to see it, so why should it be so amazing if God raises the dead? Paul simply believes what many of his colleagues in Judaism share – a belief in the resurrection.

And yet Paul is sympathetic to those who find it impossible to believe that Jesus is the one in whom the resurrection power was demonstrated. Indeed, as a good Pharisee, he became convinced that he should do everything in his power to oppose the growing influence of this man from Nazareth. And he was not happy for his opposition to be merely theoretical; he arrested and imprisoned the followers of this Nazarene and even voted for their death. He had visited many synagogues, in Judea and further afield, in order to stamp out the influence of the Christians.

Paul is trying to show that his Jewish heritage is certain and that his Jewish credentials, as a Pharisee, are impeccable. Not only that but his belief in the resurrection, the central issue at stake here (cf. 25:19; 23:6) is entirely orthodox. Jews ought to have no problems in the *possibility* of someone being raised from the dead. He then goes on to affirm how difficult it must be to accept the resurrection of Jesus – a fact he fought against 'tooth and nail' in the beginning. He really does understand their problem!

God's dramatic intervention (verses 12–23)

Paul continues with his theme of persecuting the Christians (cf. Galatians 1:13). He uses this as a 'bridge' into his conversion story: the third time Luke has recorded it for us (verses 12–18; cf. 9:1–18; 22:4–16). As usual, the basic facts are reported, with additional elements in order to communicate most effectively to this particular audience. Paul emphasizes the dramatic nature of the experience: light 'brighter than the sun' (verse 13), 'we all fell to the ground' (verse 14) and the short saying about kicking 'against the goads' (verse 14) highlight the internal struggle Paul was having. What a battle it was for this Pharisee to turn and follow Jesus!

Paul is wanting to emphasize the divine element in his call so Ananias does not get a mention. Paul is not being dishonest, simply recounting God's words without identifying the human agent who delivered them. He wants to demonstrate to this illustrious gathering that it was God *himself* who convinced him and turned his life around. This same God commissioned Paul to tell Jews and Gentiles about him: darkness would be turned to light; the devil defeated and God put in his place in people's lives; wrong things would be forgiven; and the status of being one of God's children granted to those who believed.

After this amazing encounter Paul only did what anyone would have done in these circumstances – obeyed the voice from heaven. Paul told Jew and Gentile alike that repentance was the key to spiritual life (cf. 2:38; 3:19) and that God's power would then be available to help them live in such a way as to confirm the genuineness of their repentance (cf. Matthew 3:8).

So, because he offered salvation to the Gentiles as well as the Jews, the Jews were angry with him and seized him in the temple – even trying to kill him (cf. 21:27, 31). This was the real reason for the uproar in the temple, not the trumped-up charges presented to both Felix and Festus (cf. 24:5–6; 25:7). God has been with Paul just as he promised, to help him keep on spreading the Good News. 'What's more, all this flows from the Old Testament Scriptures (e.g. Isaiah 42:6; 60:3) so I am not going against the Jews', Paul concludes. Paul wishes to be clear that he does not seek confrontation with the Jews, nor does he believe his teaching deserves their opposition.

Questions

1. Agrippa understood Judaism (verse 3). How well do we understand the 'Jewish' background to our Christian faith? How can we get to understand it better? Why is it important?
2. Paul understood those who disagreed with him. How well do we understand our non-Christian culture? What is the real reason your neighbours do not go to church? What do they really think about the Christian faith?
3. Paul's message is about forgiveness. Do we always *feel* forgiven? Why is it important to know we are forgiven? Why is it important to forgive others?

Acts 26:24-32

Paul: mad or innocent? or both?

**Paul's speech is interrupted by Festus.
Agrippa responds cautiously, but they all
know he is innocent of any crime which
deserves imprisonment or death.**

Festus interrupts (verse 24)

Festus can contain himself no longer – he
interrupts Paul in full flow. How anyone can
put his life at risk by believing that a dead man is alive seems
beyond Festus' ability to understand. He would not have
followed the logic of most of Paul's speech, but he would have
been amazed at all the fuss generated by these religious ideas.
He was a practical man and would see belief as a private thing:
hardly something to get enthusiastic about and certainly not
worth getting killed for! No wonder he thinks Paul is crazy.

Paul responds (verses 25–29)

Paul assures Festus that he is not mad, but that his words are
honest and sensible. Agrippa would be aware of the Old
Testament material and have heard about the life and ministry
of Jesus some 30 years earlier. Paul has the nerve to call Agrippa
as a witness for his position; Agrippa may well 'believe the
prophets' but he is not about to admit it publicly! Instead, he
parries Paul's question with one of his own – is Paul really trying
to persuade him to be a Christian in the course of one short
presentation of the gospel? Paul does not know how long it will
take; he just knows that he wants Agrippa and all these

influential listeners, to discover what he has, so they can be Christians like he is – apart of course from being in chains!

King and governor confer (verses 30–32)

Perhaps Agrippa is feeling convicted. The whole conversation has taken a very 'personal' turn in the last few minutes. He stands up to indicate that he considers the discussion at an end.

As King Agrippa, his sister and Governor Festus discuss the matter privately they all agree on Paul's innocence. He may be a little crazy, but he is not guilty of the charges brought against him. Agrippa is now in a better position to help Festus with his report which needs to be sent with Paul to Rome (cf. 25:26). Paul is legally innocent and on that basis could be set free, but of course it would be risky politically (see comments on 25:11) and, anyway, Paul seems determined to go to Rome. His appeal to Caesar looks like being the thing which is used to fulfil Paul's ambition (19:21) as well as God's purpose for him (23:11).

Questions

1. Do any of your non-Christian friends or neighbours think you are crazy? Why do some people find the Christian faith so difficult to believe? Is Christian faith just a 'crutch' for the psychologically weak?
2. Paul thought his faith 'true and reasonable'. Do you think your faith is reasonable? Can you defend what you believe? What evidence is there for the truth of Christianity?
3. Could you 'persuade' someone about the truth of Christianity? Can you present the gospel clearly in a couple of minutes? What are the basic elements of the Christian message which non-Christians need to hear?

Acts 27:1–26

Stormy passage

The voyage to Rome begins badly and then gets worse. Paul's advice is ignored and disaster stares them in the face.

Various views on the best course of action (verses 1–12)

After a long two-year wait, with trials under Governors Felix and Festus, Paul is at last going to Rome. He had 'appealed to Rome' (25:12), arrangements had been made and he is finally making the trip. There were a number of other prisoners who needed to be escorted under armed guard, either to Rome or one of the cities on the way, and Paul joined them aboard ship. Festus handed Paul over to Julius, giving him his written report on the situation (cf. 25:26–27).

Luke joins Paul on the ship ('we' verse 2) which is heading back to its base in Asia Minor. Aristarchus travels with them (cf. Colossians 4:10), perhaps as an aide for Paul, perhaps as another prisoner who gets converted on the voyage; we cannot know for certain. What we do know is that this section of Acts reflects Dr Luke's eyewitness account of the journey. Here we have descriptive history at its best – written up later from the journal Luke would have kept day by day. His description of the trade winds, general weather conditions, local ports, etc., is amazingly accurate – in a style almost like a modern documentary.

After a 70-mile journey north they dock at Sidon where Paul is allowed to meet with local Christians. No doubt he encouraged them in their faith just as he had at Tyre, Sidon's sister city, on his way to Jerusalem (21:3–5) and they gave him food and other necessities for a long sea voyage. On leaving Sidon they began a frustratingly slow journey north and west, the wind being in the wrong direction (verse 4). Eventually they made it to Myra, 150 miles to the north-west of Cyprus. Julius had no difficulty finding in this busy port a ship going to Italy and had his party transferred to it. Once again sailing conditions were difficult and progress very slow. A 350-mile journey – Myra to Fair Havens – apparently takes weeks, instead of days, on a route which is almost twice the normal distance.

As autumn becomes winter (the day of Atonement had passed so they may have been sailing in October) sailing becomes hazardous in this part of the Mediterranean. Paul advises them to wait in port but the owner obviously wishes to deliver his cargo promptly (time is money) and the pilot thinks it may be risky but not impossible. They decide to sail for Crete, and harbour there for the winter.

Depending on God in the tempest (verses 13–26)

Paul was a seasoned traveller with some experience of Mediterranean conditions. Despite this, his advice was over-ruled by an impatient ship-owner and an over-optimistic pilot. A light breeze from the south tempted them out of the harbour, along the Crete coast ... straight into a hurricane! They were completely at its mercy, driven south and west across the sea towards Africa. They managed to drag the small lifeboat which they were towing on board, thanks to some shelter from a little island.

Once away from the island, back in the full force of the hurricane, they secure the ship as best they can. The cargo is tossed overboard and a day later they even get rid of all the ship's equipment which was not absolutely essential. It was not possible to get their bearings from the sun or stars which were blotted out by the storm and even the most experienced sailor had given up hope.

Paul must have shared the general view that things were

pretty bleak, although he would have been trying to hold on to what he believed God had promised him (23:11). In confirmation of this an angel appears to him, repeating God's promise and also guaranteeing the safety of all the crew and passengers. The apostle, encouraged and strengthened by the angelic visitation, stands to speak to his travelling companions. He begins with a little self-congratulatory crowing ('I told you so'!) and then tells them not to lose heart. The ship will be destroyed, but none of them will lose their lives. The angel has assured Paul about this fact, along with the certainty of his ultimate arrival in Rome.

Paul is no stranger to angelic visits, visions and supernatural experiences which provide guidance and assurance for him (cf. 16:9; 18:9; 23:11). He knows that these words can be relied on – what has been said will happen! It is this certainty and deep dependency on God which marks Paul out from all around him. Twice he urges them to keep up their courage, not on the basis of his sea-faring knowledge but on the basis of his confidence in God. They put their trust in this even when they did get *shipwrecked* on an island.

Questions

1. Luke tells what he sees. Do you think this is a reliable account? How do you know that the Bible, in general, is accurate and reliable? Why is its accuracy important?
2. This journey must have frustrated Paul. How do you cope when progress (in church? at work?) is slower than you want? Why is patience so essential in the Christian life? How can we develop patience?
3. God can be relied on to do what he says. How can we remind ourselves about this? Why do we find it so hard to trust God? What other Bible passages show us how trustworthy God is?

Shipwreck and salvation

The ship is driven aground by the storm and destroyed, despite all the efforts to save it. Everyone makes it safely to the shore, and Paul has a healing ministry.

The voyagers face disaster (verses 27–44)

The storm had been raging for about two weeks when the sailors began to feel that they were approaching land. Their suspicions proved accurate when they took soundings of the water's depth; they quickly found themselves with less than 30 metres beneath them. Not wanting to be driven onto rocks, especially at night, they threw four anchors from the stern and prayed for the dawn to break. The sailors selfishly planned to abandon their passengers to a watery grave, getting away themselves in the lifeboat. Paul knew that when daylight came all the skill of the sailors would be needed to navigate the ship closer to the shore. He alerted Julius to the danger and their cowardly desertion was thwarted. This time the centurion follows Paul's advice (cf. verse 11).

Paul urges them to eat some food. Panic and pressure of work (not to mention sea-sickness!) had left them all very weak. They will need strength for the swim to shore. Paul takes some food, says grace, and begins to eat. Encouraged by this example they all have a meal and then throw everything else which can be moved over the side. They will need the ship to be as light as possible for the difficult approach to land. With 276 people on board there is enough human weight without needing to carry any 'excess luggage'.

When light comes they can see land but they do not recognize it; there is a sandy shore-line where it may be possible to land safely. They let the sea keep the four anchors they had tossed out the night before, hoisted a small sail and tried to run aground on the beach. They actually struck a sand-bar, got stuck with the bow trapped in the muddy sand beneath the surface and the ship began to break up. The soldiers wanted to kill the prisoners, but Julius is especially keen to save Paul so prevents this occurring. As the stern of the ship breaks up behind them the swimmers are encouraged to get to land. The non-swimmers were to grab anything which would float and struggle to the shore, clinging to their homemade 'rafts'. Luke is quick to tell us that despite this undignified (not to say dangerous!) exit from the ship, not a single life is lost.

Life is restored (verses 1–10)

The ship had been blown about 500 miles west from its last harbour, Fair Havens, and arrived at the island of Malta. There would have been great relief at their escape from the hurricane, but some anxiety about whether or not the natives on this strange island would be friendly. They were! A large fire was built by them to help the 276 casualties avoid the consequences of exposure on a very wet and cold morning. Paul, despite his leadership role among them and the prophetic insight which had assured them of their safety, helps collect wood for the fire. He does not assume any airs and graces or refuse to help practically because of his position or status. As he served in this humble way a snake sank its fangs into Paul's hand.

The snake had obviously been asleep (or close to death from the cold?) and disturbed by the heat from the fire had roused itself to strike at Paul. The superstitious islanders saw divine judgment in this – he may have escaped what the gods had in store for him at sea, but their plans cannot be thwarted; they send a snake to kill him on land. Paul, however, shakes this poisonous snake off into the fire and is unharmed. The people watch this 'murderer' for hours to see if the poison will take effect and when it does not they assume that the 'murderer' is in fact a 'god' (cf. 14:11–13).

Once all the 276 are accounted for, the governor of the island, Publius, welcomes them on to his estate until accommodation can be found on the island. This process of providing food and lodging for 276 people for the winter months takes three days – a remarkably efficient operation.

The father of Publius had been confined to bed with a serious illness (perhaps 'Malta fever', from a virus found in goats' milk on the island); Paul volunteered to pray with the sick man, and he was healed. This miracle prompted others to bring their sick friends to Paul, possibly also to doctor Luke, and he exercised a significant healing ministry on the island. Despite all the tiredness from the long journey to Rome, a strange island, an exhausting storm, a brush with death in the shipwreck and the snake-bite . . . Paul is still ready to be used by God. No wonder the islanders were so generous when the time came to leave!

Questions

1. Paul told them to eat (verse 33). This does not seem very 'spiritual' advice! Is 'practical' the opposite of 'spiritual'? Shouldn't he have told them to pray? How can Christians develop this 'feet-on-the-ground' common sense?

2. The passage describes kindness to strangers. Who are the strangers in our community? Would you use your home for homeless people on a temporary basis? Would you let someone borrow your car? Share your food? Take your coat? (cf. Luke 6:30–31).

3. Notice Paul's humility. Why is humility so important? Why do we like to be noticed? How can we kill our pride, and so become usable by God.

Acts 28:11–22

Paul in Rome

**After spending the winter on Malta, Julius and his
prisoners set sail for Italy. Paul is warmly welcomed
throughout southern Italy, and arrives safely
in Rome, where he meets the Jewish leaders.**

A Christian welcome (verses 11–16)

It was extremely difficult for sailing ships in
the winter months in this part of the Mediterranean. Weather conditions would have made a journey
before February close to impossible. Julius would have been
keen to get his prisoners to Rome, but not keen enough to want
to face another storm! They probably left Malta during early
February and made their way on an Egyptian ship to Sicily, 80
miles to the north. Luke draws our attention to the figurehead
which represented Gemini. These 'heavenly twins' were supposed to protect from storm and disaster at sea. Paul must have
had a wry smile when he saw this maritime good-luck charm; he
would continue to put his trust in a God who really could
protect from storms (cf. 27:24)!

The journey to Syracuse was completed in a day, but a
combination of bad weather and unloading of cargo kept them
in port for another 72 hours. When a favourable south wind
arrived they travelled to Rhegium, a harbour in the 'toe' of Italy,
and on the next day set off on the 180-mile journey up the coast
to Puteoli. At this point Paul's journey by boat came to an end –
just 140 miles short of his final destination.

Puteoli was a significant city and already had a small number
of Christians. They were not slow in welcoming Paul to their city,

and a week was spent together in teaching, fellowship and encouragement (cf. brothers in Sidon; 27:3). News of Paul's arrival in Italy had reached the church in Rome and they sent a delegation to give Paul a hero's welcome. About 43 miles from Rome at the Forum of Appius and again 33 miles from Rome at Three Taverns there are scenes of joy, greeting, welcome and fellowship. Julius must have been amazed by all this. He already knew that Paul was no ordinary prisoner, but the strength of Christian brotherhood (between people who had never met!) would have staggered him. Paul is delighted and strengthened by all this love from Italian Christians.

Paul finally arrived in Rome and was allowed to live on his own, in his own accommodation, though guarded by a soldier. This special treatment was no doubt obtained because of Paul's Roman citizenship, the positive nature of the letter from Festus and the glowing tribute that must have come from Julius. This mild form of house arrest gave him great freedom.

A respectful hearing (verses 17–22)

After just three days in Rome Paul wishes to put his case before the leading Jews in the city. It was his custom to visit the synagogue as soon as he arrived in a town (cf. 13:14; 14:1), but his house arrest made this very difficult; on this occasion they would have to come to him. Using the normal greeting of 'men, brothers', he begins to explain his presence in Rome to them. He is anxious to reassure them about his loyalty as a Jew. He has not done anything to damage the Jewish people or been deliberately acting against the established traditions. Despite this he was arrested in Jerusalem and tried by the Romans, though they came to believe he was innocent of any significant crime (cf. 25:7; 26:31–32).

When the Jews in Judea were resistant to Paul's freedom he felt that he had to invoke his right as a Roman citizen to be tried by Caesar. He is at pains to point out that this was simply to protect his own life, not to bring a counter-charge against the Jews. Paul believes that his presence in Rome is due to a disagreement about the 'hope of Israel', that is, a dispute relating to the Messiah. Every Jew looked forward to the day when God's great deliverer would come, it was a completely orthodox expectation. The difference between Paul and his accusers was that he believed that this 'hope' had been fulfilled in Jesus, and they did not.

In response to this initial explanation, the leaders of the Jewish community say that they have had no correspondence from Jerusalem about him and that Jewish visitors to Rome have not brought any negative reports to them. This is difficult to believe even with slow communication in the ancient world. Perhaps they are being incredibly diplomatic because they feel very vulnerable in Rome as a mistrusted minority. Perhaps they want to maintain a low profile and not get involved in any controversy. Paul can never have been treated so respectfully by Jewish leaders!

Whatever the reasons for their non-hostile response they are curious to hear first-hand from this Christian missionary. Everyone seems to be talking about Christianity and they are keen to discover what the fuss is all about.

Questions

1. Paul had support from other Christians. In what ways is the help we get from other Christians different from any help we might get from non-Christians? How can Christians who have never met before have such close relationships so quickly?
2. Paul has not been disloyal to his Jewish heritage. Why is loyalty so important to him? How do we demonstrate loyalty – to Christ? To the church? To our partner? To the family? To our country?
3. Paul claimed Jesus was the Messiah. Why do you think this was hard for the Jews to believe? What Old Testament passages point to Jesus as the Messiah? How would you go about persuading a Jew about Jesus today?

Acts 28:23–31

The gospel is preached

Paul explains his position fully to the Jewish leaders. There is a mixed response. Paul continues to preach to everyone who will listen!

The leaders of the Jews arranged to come back to hear Paul on a more convenient occasion. When they returned the delegation had increased in size; interest in this 'Christian', this leading light of a new 'sect' was obviously substantial. Paul must have been staying in some spacious accommodation in order to entertain them all. For a whole day he tried to persuade them about life in God's kingdom. This was also the theme of the risen Jesus to the first disciples (1:3). He worked hard to demonstrate that Moses and the Prophets had all pointed to Jesus as Messiah; that he was not a believer in a new religion, simply that he was enjoying what God had promised would happen.

It would have been a great delight to Paul that some of these men of authority in the Jewish synagogue came to faith in Christ (cf. Crispus in 18:8). Of course there were some who refused to believe because of stubbornly closed minds . . . and perhaps the majority were just unsure what to make of it all. Certainly there was division among them, just as there had been at the Sanhedrin trial in Jerusalem (23:9). The final straw for many of them came when Paul made his closing two points.

Firstly, he quoted Isaiah 6:9 to them. The prophets had always known how stubborn the Jews would be and how they would fail to recognize the Messiah. Secondly, this meant that Paul now had the freedom to take his message to the Gentiles, so that they could enjoy all the benefits of God's salvation (cf. 9:15; 13:46–48).

This was more than these Jews could take and they slipped out before they heard anything even more shocking.

For two years Paul was allowed to live comfortably in his rented accommodation and had no problem in receiving visitors whenever they came. Luke concludes his book with a verse of encouragement and confidence. Paul's physical confinement did not mean that the preaching of the gospel was inhibited. Far from it. He was able to speak without fear, boldly explaining his beliefs and pointing his visitors to the Jesus who was both Lord and Christ (2:36). This truth was proclaimed to Jew and Gentile alike. It was a message which would be preached all over the world (1:8) until the Jesus Paul loved returned (1:11).

Questions

1. Are there any individuals (or groups of people) who we do not really want to hear the gospel (cf. 'Gentiles')? Should we evangelize people of other religions or just those with no faith? Do we need foreign missionaries any more? Why?
2. Paul received a mixed response. What kind of response do we get? What should the church do to encourage those who believe? How can we respond to those who don't. Should we move on to other people or keep trying?
3. Paul took every opportunity to evangelize. Why was evangelism such a priority for him? How can we make it more of a priority for ourselves? Why should we? How can we go about it?

Whatever happened to Paul?

Nobody knows the answer to this question although there have been many attempts to discover the truth. Some believe that at the end of the two years (28:30) Paul was tried by Caesar and then executed. But if this is so it is hard to explain Luke's silence about the matter and harder still to explain some of the material in Paul's letters, particularly the letters to Timothy.

Paul was probably freed after two years because the case against him was weak (26:31–32) and his accusers had failed to turn up in Rome. He thought he might get thrown to the lions, but avoided this fate (2 Timothy 4:17) and may have had the opportunity to revisit some of the churches he had planted. He may even have made his way to Spain, fulfilling a strong desire to preach the gospel there (Romans 15:24, 28). He could well have been re-arrested at a time when the Roman authorities were less sympathetic to Christianity (e.g. after the great fire of Rome in AD 64 which Emperor Nero blamed the Christians for starting). It seems most likely that Paul was martyred between AD 65–68 in the Nero-inspired persecutions.

Further reading

John R. W. Stott, *The message of Acts*, The Bible Speaks Today (IVP, Eerdmans, 1990).
I. Howard Marshall, *Acts*, Tyndale New Testament Commentary (IVP, 1980).

EPHESIANS

Stephen Motyer

Free to be one

Crossway Bible Guides

Paul urges the Ephesian church to be at one; to be a place:

* ⋆ of strength for spiritual warfare
* ⋆ where relationships are transformed by God's grace and peace
* ⋆ where wholeness of living is vibrantly expressed

Crossway Bible Guides are designed for personal devotion and for group study leaders and members. They give a concise summary and lively application of each passage. They help us grasp the message of the Bible, and, more important, help the Bible get a grip on us.

A useful resource for personal Bible reading and group studies –

Michael Green

Evangelical Alliance is delighted to join together with Crossway in publishing this new series –

Clive Calver

Individuals or groups could find great benefit from this series. Major points are highlighted followed by uncompromising and sharp questions –

Donald English

These guides will facilitate, stimulate and enrich your discovery of God's Word –

Roger Forster

Steve Motyer taught at Oak Hill College and spent four years as a country vicar before becoming a lecturer in New Testament at London Bible College in 1987. He is a respected speaker, and author of *Israel in the Plan of God* and *Unlocking the Bible* (S.U.). He lives in Watford with his wife Val, their three children and a collection of tropical fish.

HOUSEGROUPS

the leaders' survival guide

Editors: Ian Coffey and Stephen Gaukroger

Ever since New Testament times small groups of Christians have met to learn, to worship and to grow together. Housegroups have enjoyed great popularity in the last few decades, and much experience and wisdom in leading them has been distilled by the authors of this book.

Are you thinking of starting a housegroup or taking your existing group forward? Or has your group gone a little flat? *Housegroups: the leaders' survival guide* will give you the vision you are looking for:

* ★ What's the point of housegroups?
* ★ What makes a good leader?
* ★ Teaching the Bible in small groups
* ★ Prayer, worship and evangelism
* ★ Troubleshooter's guide and much more

Authors include Peter Meadows, John Earwicker, Dave Cave, Steve Motyer, Nick Mercer, Chris Bowater.

Editors Stephen Gaukroger and Ian Coffey are both senior ministers in Baptist churches and series editors of the Crossway Bible Guides. They share with the other authors a contagious enthusiasm for housegroups.

1 PETER

Andrew Whitman

Free to hope

Crossway Bible Guides

The apostle Peter encourages us to have hope in all circumstances because

★ God's love for us is sure
★ God is always in control
★ God is in charge of the future

Crossway Bible Guides are designed for personal devotion and for group-study leaders and members. They give a concise summary and lively application of each passage. They help us grasp the message of the Bible, and more important, help the Bible get a grip on us.

A useful resource for personal Bible reading and group studies –
Michael Green

Evangelical Alliance is delighted to join together with Crossway in publishing this new series –
Clive Calver

Individuals or groups could find great benefit from this series. Major points are highlighted followed by uncompromising and sharp questions –
Donald English

These guides will facilitate, stimulate and enrich your discovery of God's Word –
Roger Forster

Andrew Whitman is the pastor of Godmanchester Baptist Church, near Huntingdon, where he lives with his family.

TIMOTHY AND TITUS

Michael Griffiths

Train for discipleship

Crossway Bible Guides

Paul wrote twice to Timothy and once to Titus, equipping them to:

* ★ make true disciples
* ★ detect and eliminate false teaching
* ★ appoint and encourage church elders and overseers
* ★ clarify the roles of men and women in leadership

The problems which often face our churches today are strikingly similar to those met in first-century Ephesus and Crete. These letters were written for us.

Crossway Bible Guides are tailor-made for group study leaders and members and are also ideal for personal devotional use. They provide a concise summary and lively application of each passage, with pointed questions to probe more deeply into personal, church-centred and global issues. They help us to grasp the Bible's message and the Bible to get a grip on us.

A useful resource for personal Bible Reading and group studies –
Michael Green

Evangelical Alliance is delighted to join together with Crossway in publishing this new series –
Clive Calver

Individuals or groups could find great benefit from this series. Major points are highlighted followed by uncompromising and sharp questions –
Donald English

These guides will facilitate, stimulate and enrich your discovery of God's Word –
Roger Forster

Michael Griffiths is a widely respected conference speaker and author who, like Timothy, delights in making disciples. A former Director of the Overseas Missionary Fellowship and Principal of London Bible College, he is now a freelance Christian lecturer and writer.